D1717149

THE LIBRARY OF
AMERICAN
LIVES AND TIMES™

POCAHONTAS

The Powhatan Culture and the Jamestown Colony

Lisa Sita

The Rosen Publishing Group's
PowerPlus Books™

To my family

Published in 2005 by The Rosen Publishing Group, Inc.
29 East 21st Street, New York, NY 10010

First Edition

*Editor's Note: All quotations have been reproduced as they appeared in
the letters and diaries from which they were borrowed. No correction was
made to the inconsistent spelling that was common in that time period.*

Library of Congress Cataloging-in-Publication Data

Sita, Lisa, 1962–
Pocahontas : the Powhatan culture and the Jamestown Colony / Lisa Sita.
      v. cm. — (The library of American lives and times)
Includes bibliographical references and index.
Contents: The nonpareil of Virginia — The Powhatan Indians —
Before Jamestown — Culture conflict — The struggle to survive in
Jamestown — Did Pocahontas rescue John Smith? — Rising tensions
— Pocahontas is kidnapped — Pocahontas and John Rolfe — The
Virginia Colony continues to grow — Conclusion.
ISBN 1-4042-2653-2 (lib. bdg.)
1. Pocahontas, d. 1617—Juvenile literature. 2. Powhatan women—
Biography—Juvenile literature. 3. Powhatan Indians—Social life and
customs. 4. Smith, John, 1580–1631—Juvenile literature. 5.
Jamestown (Va.)—History—Juvenile literature. 6. Virginia—History—
Colonial period, ca. 1600–1775—Juvenile literature. [1. Pocahontas, d.
1617. 2. Powhatan Indians—Biography. 3. Indians of North America—
Virginia—Biography. 4. Women—Biography. 5. Smith, John,
1580–1631. 6. Jamestown (Va.)—History. 7. Virginia—History—
Colonial period, ca. 1600–1775.] I. Title. II. Series.

E99.P85.P5793 2005
975.5'01'092—dc22

                                          2003024456

Manufactured in the United States of America

CONTENTS

Ætalis suæ 21. Aº. 1616.

1. The Nonpareil of Virginia

On December 20, 1606, the *Susan Constant*, *Discovery*, and *Godspeed* set sail from England carrying cargo, 40 crewmen, and 104 passengers, all of them men and boys. The ships reached North America in the spring of 1607 and sailed up the James River in Virginia. On May 13, the expedition moored off an island they named James Island. The expedition had arrived at a place where the passengers were to establish a colony called Jamestown, named for King James I, who was then the king of England. Jamestown was the first permanent English settlement in America.

In their first few years in Jamestown, the settlers were plagued with hunger and sickness. They came to rely on the local Native Americans to provide them with food. Over time, however, the generally friendly relationship between the English and the Native Americans changed to one of hostility and warfare.

Opposite: This portrait of Pocahontas was based on a 1616 engraving done by Simon van de Passe during Pocahontas's visit to England. The leaders of the Virginia Company, who founded the Jamestown Colony, brought Pocahontas to England. The company funded her trip to publicize their business activities in North America.

Between 1607 and 1609, the English captain John Smith and Chief Powhatan, a Native American leader, would play major roles in the story of Jamestown, as would Powhatan's favorite daughter, Pocahontas.

Pocahontas was probably born in 1595. Early records estimate her age to have been anywhere from ten to twelve when she first met the Jamestown colonists. At that time, Powhatan was the most powerful ruler of all the Indian tribal groups in his region. Together these groups were known as the Powhatan Indians. The Indians did not keep written records at that time. Therefore, what we know of Pocahontas's life and times comes mostly from the written accounts of the Englishmen of Jamestown. Archaeological finds, including artifacts, human and animal bones, and traces of where shelters once stood, also contribute to our understanding of this period.

John Smith was the first person to write about Pocahontas in his account *True Relation*, written in 1608. He describes how Pocahontas was sent by her father on a mission to Jamestown to negotiate peace with the colonists. This was Pocahontas's first visit to Jamestown. According to Smith, Pocahontas was a spirited, intelligent girl. He described her as "a childe of tenne yeares old, which not only for feature, [bearing], and proportion, much exceedeth any of the rest of [Powhatan's] people, but for wit, and spirit, the only Nonpareil of his country."

The interaction of Pocahontas and John Smith in the 1600s still fascinates artists and the public more than four centuries later. This print was an illustration in a 1906 children's book *The Story of Pocahontas and Captain Smith,* which was written and illustrated by Elmer Boyd Smith.

The word "nonpareil" means someone who stands out above the rest, or someone who is unequaled. Powhatan himself favored Pocahontas, although he had many other children by several different wives. Some of the colonists described Pocahontas as "Powhatan's dearest daughter."

In Powhatan culture, people usually had more than one name, and each name had a meaning. Pocahontas was a nickname in the Powhatan language that was translated by the English of the seventeenth century as

The wife of a Native American chief and her daughter were drawn by the English artist and explorer John White around 1585. The child holds a doll that was made in England.

"wanton," which in modern English means "frolicsome," or one who is playful and mischievous. A Powhatan child's first name was given a few days after his or her birth, when family members gathered for a celebration. The father would hold the baby in his arms and declare the child's name. This ceremony was followed by feasting and dancing. Later, children would receive other, less formal, names and these would be the names by which they were commonly called.

Pocahontas's formal name was Matoaka. According to some scholars, this name comes from a word in the Powhatan language meaning "she enjoys playing with others."

Although Pocahontas first went to Jamestown as a messenger for her father, she often returned to visit.

Bright and energetic, she enjoyed playing with the English children. In appearance Pocahontas was much like other Powhatan girls. She did not wear any clothes until she reached puberty, which was the Powhatan custom. Pocahontas also had the typical hairstyle of a Powhatan girl and wore her hair cut short and close to her head, except for a braid in back. One of the Jamestown colonists, William Strachey, described how Pocahontas played with the boys in the town. She would "make them wheele, falling on their handes turning their heels upwards." Once the boys had learned how to do this, the children would cartwheel all around the fort.

In John Smith's book *Generall Historie of Virginia*, written in 1624, Smith tells the story of how Pocahontas saved his life. Some modern scholars doubt that the rescue ever took place. However, whether or not the story is true, Pocahontas remains a key figure in American history. Through her kindness and compassion, she helped the settlers of Jamestown to survive, by bringing them food from her father, and by assisting in the establishment of good relations between the English colonists and the Powhatan Indians.

2. The Powhatan Indians

The Powhatan Indians lived in the Chesapeake Bay region of present-day Virginia and Maryland. Scholars estimate that when the English arrived in 1607, there were between 8,000 and 14,000 Powhatans residing in the area. The Powhatan nation was composed of several different tribes. All of the tribes spoke a dialect of Algonquian, the family of languages spoken by many Native Americans living along the eastern coast of North America. The Powhatans arc also known as the Virginia Algonquians or the Tidewater Indians.

"Tidewater" refers to the environment in which the Powhatans lived. The Virginia Tidewater is a coastal plain, an area of low-lying land on the coast of the Atlantic Ocean. The Chesapeake Bay, situated on the Atlantic coast, forms an estuary, or a body of water where the salt water of the ocean and the freshwater of

Opposite: This photograph of Jamestown Island, which is situated in the James River, offers a bird's-eye view of the trees that are native to this marshy coastal region of Virginia. Among the trees that have flourished in the Virginia Tidewater are oak, red maple, black gum, bald cypress, and loblolly pine.

The Secotan Indians lived in the coastal region of North Carolina and sustained themselves by hunting and farming. John White's 1585 watercolor of a Secotan village documented the villagers' cultivation of crops, which included corn, sunflowers, pumpkins, and tobacco.

rivers meet. Five major rivers flow into the bay. The rivers are the Potomac, the Rappahannock, the York, the James, and the Susquehanna, with several smaller rivers and creeks branching off from them. The entire area includes beaches, marshlands, swamps, and forests. The range of land inhabited by the Powhatans spanned about 100 miles (161 km) from east to west, from the Atlantic Ocean to the fall line, or a place where the Indians could no longer travel the rivers because of waterfalls. From north to south, approximately between the present-day borders of Maryland and North Carolina, the Powhatan homeland stretched along the coast for another 100 miles (161 km).

The Powhatans built their villages along the banks of the rivers. The rivers and their streams offered water for drinking and bathing and provided food such as fish, oysters, and mussels. The rivers were also important for transportation by dugout canoe, allowing people to communicate and trade with one another all along the waterways. The canoes were made from a single log that was split in half and hollowed out by gradually burning the inside of the log and then scraping out the burnt wood.

The Powhatans constructed their homes by fastening mats made from rushes or strips of bark over an arched framework of cut saplings. An opening was left at either end of the home for entrances and in the roof, as well, so that smoke from the household fire could escape. Inside this shelter, low wooden platforms covered with mats served as beds. Household utensils included dishes and cups made from turtle shells, ladles and spoons made from gourds and shells, clay cooking pots, and wooden mortars and pestles that were used to grind corn. Other furnishings, which were usually made from plant materials, included mats, bags, and baskets for gathering and storing food.

Women grew food in the fields, which were located near the homes. To clear the ground for planting, the Powhatans practiced slash-and-burn agriculture. They removed the trees in an area by burning them and then clearing them away. The remains of large tree stumps were left in place and the crops were grown among them.

Corn was the most important and valued food that the Powhatans harvested, although they also grew beans and squash. Using a digging stick to poke holes in the ground, women dropped a few seeds of corn and beans together into each hole. As the crops came up, the cornstalks would support the vines of the growing beans. Squashes, gourds, and pumpkins were planted between the rows of corn and beans. Boys and girls often helped the women in the gardens by sowing the seeds and weeding. Children also kept watch and scared off birds and other wildlife that could eat the seeds and the young plants. Pocahontas might have helped the women in her village in such a way.

Besides growing food, women also gathered plants from the land. Wild berries and nuts were collected to

Shown above are some of the foods that were essential to the Powhatans' diet. Included on the mat are squashes, pumpkins, corn, and several varieties of beans

be eaten. Oils from some nuts were used to prepare certain medications.

In addition to providing plants, the Tidewater region offered a wide variety of animals that the Powhatans used for food and for raw materials. Men usually fished from canoes using several different methods. They caught fish in nets, snagged them using fishing lines with bone hooks, stabbed the fish with spears, or caught them in traps called weirs. The men also gathered shellfish by diving for them. The men hunted for deer and wild turkeys, as well as for

This 1585 watercolor by John White shows the various methods that Native Americans from the coastal region of Virginia used to catch fish. To lure fish to the surface during the night, men would light a small fire in their canoes.

other animals such as raccoon, opossums, beavers, otters, turtles, and snakes.

A Powhatan man's reputation depended on his hunting ability, as well as on his skills as a warrior, so boys were taught these skills at a very young age. Methods of hunting varied. Hunters caught smaller animals in traps. They hunted larger animals with bows and arrows. Bears were killed for their meat, their fur, and for their fat, which was mixed with crushed minerals to make paint. Deer were trapped in different ways. Sometimes a hunter wearing a deerskin stalked the animal before shooting it with a bow and arrow. To hunt a herd of deer, several men surrounded the animals and trapped them. They did this by building fires around them or by driving them into the water where other hunters waiting in canoes shot them.

The deer were then brought to the women of the village, who skinned them and prepared the carcasses for a variety of uses. Deer provided meat for food; bones for making tools and utensils; sinew, or muscle tendon, for string; and skins for clothing. The women scraped the skins and then tanned, or preserved, them before sewing them into garments.

Pocahontas and other young girls observed the women in their village carrying out such tasks. Eventually, after watching the adults work, the girls would imitate the women and undertake these activities themselves. As the daughter of a chief, Pocahontas

This watercolor, based on a 1585 drawing by John White, shows stew cooking in the type of pot used by the Powhatans. The pot was made from layers of clay coils molded together.

probably had more leisure time than did most other girls her age.

Powhatan clothing included fringed leather aprons for women and loincloths for men. In the forest, where brambles and branches could scratch their skin, the Powhatans wore deerskin leggings and moccasins. Both men and women wore jewelry and body paint. Hairstyles for both sexes could be quite elaborate. Women also tattooed their bodies with designs of flowers and animals.

The Powhatans made all the tools they used from stone and other natural materials. Arrowheads and axes were made from quartz and flint, sharpened reeds, bird bills, beaver teeth, and sharpened shells. When the English arrived with metal axes, hatchets, and firearms, the Powhatans were eager to trade for these tools and weapons, which were sturdier and stronger than their own.

Powhatan families had all they needed in their sur- roundings to care for themselves and were quite self- sufficient. Yet some families were wealthier than others. The wealthier Powhatans had more luxury items, such as copper, shell beads, and freshwater pearls, many of which they acquired through trade. The most impor- tant method of becoming wealthy, however, was by hav- ing a large supply of food. To be wealthy, a man had to be a good hunter. He also needed a great deal of corn and other foods that women produced. Therefore, in Powhatan culture it was desirable to have more than one wife. To have sev- eral wives, a man had to prove himself as an able provider and protector. Powhatan women did not want to marry men who could not provide for them and defend them. The more wives a man could attract, the more food he could bring into his household through the women's farming and gathering.

Child rearing was a com- munal task for Powhatan women. Mothers watched and cared for children, as did grandmothers, older sis- ters, and aunts.

Virginian Powhatans made this bag from deerskin. They decorated it with shell beads. The bag was brought to England in 1614.

When a child was born, it was customary to dip the baby in water, regardless of how cold the water was. Powhatans of all ages bathed every morning, even in the winter months. The Powhatans bathed not only for cleanliness, but also because the practice was believed to keep the people hardy in all kinds of weather.

Until they were able to crawl, babies spent their infancy bound to wooden boards called cradle-boards. Wrapped in skins and then strapped to these boards with a cord, the babies could be carried or hung from a tree branch as the women did their daily work.

Pocahontas's childhood was probably spent much like that of other wealthy Powhatan children. She learned the skills she would need as an adult and played with the other children in her town. Although much is known of Pocahontas's father, little is known of her mother. Pocahontas's

This Native American woman, drawn by John White in 1585, has tattoos on her legs. Circles, triangles, and designs of flowers, fruits, and snakes were often used to decorate the body.

mother was one of Powhatan's many wives. Chief Powhatan was said to have had more than one hundred wives from different towns. Most of these women lived with their own people. Powhatan had a total of at least twenty sons and ten daughters with these women.

After one of Powhatan's wives had borne a child, Powhatan sent the woman back to her town with the baby. There the mother would raise the child until Powhatan was ready to have his son or daughter returned to him to be raised in his household. By the time the English arrived, Pocahontas was living apart from her mother.

As a girl living in her father's village, Pocahontas would also join in the feasting that the Powhatans enjoyed on special occasions. These celebrations included a great deal of singing and dancing. Dancing was both an important part of Powhatan rituals and a favored leisure activity in the evening after the day's work was done.

The Powhatan nation was a chiefdom, which meant that it was composed of several towns or villages that were all under the rule of a single chief, or leader. Powhatan, Pocahontas's father, was the paramount, or the supreme chief, of the Indian groups in his region. As the highest-ranking ruler, he was known as Powhatan, but his personal name was Wahunsenacawh. The Algonquian word for his rank as the supreme chief was *mamanatowick*. Powhatan held great power over the

A Secotan Indian dance, probably in celebration of the corn harvest, was recorded by John White around 1585 in the coastal region of North Carolina. As they danced around a circle of carved wooden posts, men and women carried small leafy branches and rattles made from gourds.

people of his region and his people paid Powhatan tribute by giving him deerskins, food, and other valuables.

Powhatan's chiefdom was made up of districts. Each district was ruled by a lesser chief who was called in Algonquian *weroance*, or *weroansqua* if the chief was a woman. Each district had several towns within it, and each town also had a leader. The town leaders were called weroances as well. The town weroances had to answer to the weroance of their district, and the district weroances had to answer to the mamanatowick

Powhatan. All these leaders expected obedience and respect from those whom they led.

Other important members of Powhatan society were the *quiyoughcosuck*, or priests. The Powhatans believed that priests had special abilities as seers, or individuals who could look into the future and predict the outcome of events. For this reason, priests had great influence over their rulers and were often consulted in matters of warfare.

One dramatic example of the power of priests occurred sometime around 1607. Powhatan's priests told him that a nation from the Chesapeake Bay would arise to "dissolve and give end to his Empire." Powhatan decided that the group to which the seers were referring was a tribe called the Chesapeake. Therefore, he had all the Chesapeake people killed.

It was also thought that priests could identify people who had committed

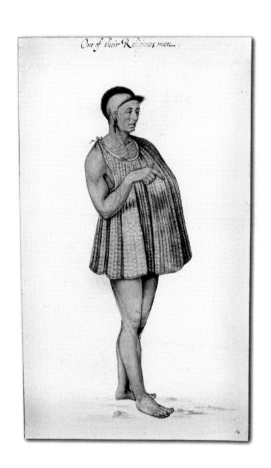

John White drew this Native American priest around 1585. Powhatans believed priests protected the crops by controlling the weather.

crimes. Punishment for certain crimes was severe. Anyone who robbed or murdered another Powhatan, or who helped to commit such crimes, was executed. However, it was not considered a crime to steal from or to kill anyone who was not a Powhatan.

Men who were exceptionally skilled hunters and warriors also held a high place among the Powhatan, although they were not as powerful as the priests were. The rulers respected hunters and warriors and sought their advice because of their skills.

3. Before Jamestown

The paramount chiefdom that Chief Powhatan eventually created began as a smaller chiefdom that he had inherited from his ancestors in the mid-to-late 1500s. Powhatan's chiefdom grew as he conquered more groups, such as the Nansemond, the Weyanock, and the Warraskoyack. By 1607, Powhatan ruled all the tribes in the Chesapeake Bay area except for the Chickahominy, a large tribe that he could not conquer.

During the period when Powhatan enlarged his chiefdom, the kings and queens of Europe expanded their empires around the world. Trade was thriving and items from Asia, such as exotic spices and silks, were brought to Europe to be sold as luxury goods in European markets.

Early trade routes from Europe to Asia were mostly over land. By the end of the fifteenth century, however, monarchs were hiring explorers to find faster and shorter passages by sea. A turning point came when the Portuguese explorer Vasco da Gama discovered a new sea route to Asia. He sailed from Portugal, around the Cape of Good Hope in Africa, and into the

POWHATAN

Appamatuck

This depiction of Chief Powhatan was part of John Smith's 1608 map of Virginia, which Willam Hole engraved in 1612. William Hole probably based this engraving on several sources. He may have used earlier works that were done by John White and Theodore De Bry, as well as John Smith's eyewitness account of his captivity among Powhatans in 1607.

Indian Ocean, where he eventually reached India.

Interest was also keen for trading ventures in the Americas. After Christopher Columbus had sailed to the West Indies in 1492, the Americas became known as the New World. European interest in the New World was fueled by the desire for trade with the native peoples and the exploitation of natural resources, such as gold and other precious metals. During this initial period of global exploration, people did not know a great deal about the geography of the world. European monarchs were hopeful that somewhere in the New World was yet another profitable trade route to Asia.

The journey to and from Europe and America was long and dangerous. Voyages took several months or longer, depending on the weather at sea. Therefore, it was common for countries such as Spain, England, Portugal, the Netherlands, and England to establish colonies in the Americas where their people could live and set up trade and business ventures with merchants in Europe. It was also common practice for Europeans to kidnap native youths and then teach them European languages. Once these native children were taught the language of the explorers, they often served as interpreters for the Europeans in their business dealings with the local peoples.

The first Europeans to visit the Chesapeake Bay area were Spanish and Portuguese explorers. Their goal was to

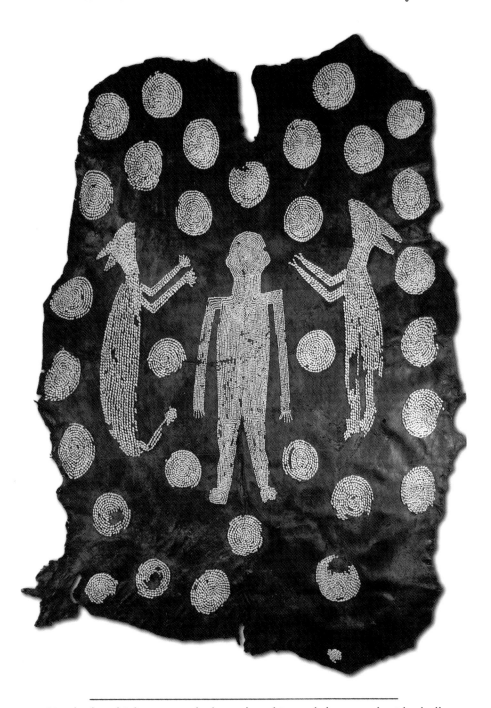

This cloak, which was made from deerskin and decorated with shells, is believed to have been worn by Chief Powhatan or another Native American chief in the late 1500s or early 1600s. Historians estimate that about 20,000 shells were embroidered onto this garment.

capture and enslave Native Americans, and to find a shorter route to China. Around 1560, Spain attempted to establish a colony in the region. An exploration party kidnapped an Indian boy who they later found out was a son of a Powhatan weroance. They sent the boy to Mexico and then to Cuba, both places that had been colonized by Spain. The boy was expected to learn Spanish language and customs and to become a Christian. He was baptized and named Don Luis de Velasco.

Don Luis returned to his homeland in 1570 with a group of Jesuit missionaries who established a mission

This modern watercolor by Norman Wilkinson is a representation of the 1588 Spanish Armada, Spain's fleet of warships. Spain used armed ships such as these to explore and colonize North America. Regardless of their individual destinations, the ships assembled before undertaking the dangerous crossing of the Atlantic Ocean.

on the banks of the York River. A mission is a site that is built by religious leaders with the aim of educating and converting the native population to Christianity. Don Luis left the Spanish mission to join his own people, who were suffering from a famine brought about by a drought.

Eventually, Don Luis rejected Spanish culture and Christianity. In 1571, Don Luis led an attack on the mission and killed everyone except for one Spanish boy. The boy was named Alonso. He escaped and one of the local Native American groups took him in. When a Spanish supply ship arrived later that year, the crew found only Indians at the mission site. The following year, the Spanish returned to America for a counterattack. They recovered Alonso and killed more than thirty Powhatan Indians.

In 1584, the English arrived in America hoping to start a settlement on Roanoke Island, located off the coast of present-day North Carolina. The colony was unsuccessful and the settlers returned home. In 1587, the English tried again. Sir Walter Raleigh sent three ships to Roanoke Island with a total of 117 men, women, and children to settle the area. The Roanoke Colony eventually ran low on supplies, so its leader John White went to England to replenish, or replace, the colonists' store.

John White returned in 1590 to find that the colony had vanished. Later, English colonists in the area recorded rumors that the settlers had been attacked and killed by Indians, but there is no evidence to support this. Some scholars believe that a few of the Roanoke settlers went to live with the Indians, possibly as refugees or as captives. The fate of the Roanoke settlers remains a mystery. For this reason it is known as the Lost Colony of Roanoke.

The colony of Jamestown was settled seventeen years later, in 1607. Jamestown began with a charter granted by James I, the king of England, in April 1606. A charter is an official document granting rights or privileges from a government to an individual, a group of people, or a company. King James granted a charter for a colony to be established in Virginia. The charter also specified that Edward Maria Wingfield would serve as the colony's first president. The Virginia Company, a group of London merchants, was created to finance this venture. Eight months later, the three ships carrying the future settlers of Jamestown set sail from England. They arrived in Virginia in April of the following year.

Business was the main purpose of the enterprise. The Virginia Company instructed the colonists to explore a new route to Asia and to find natural resources, such as precious metals and timber, which could be exported to Europe. The company also wanted the colonists to convert the Indians to Christianity. This effort to convert Native Americans was common among Europeans coming to the Americas. The majority of people throughout Europe practiced Christianity and considered it the religion of

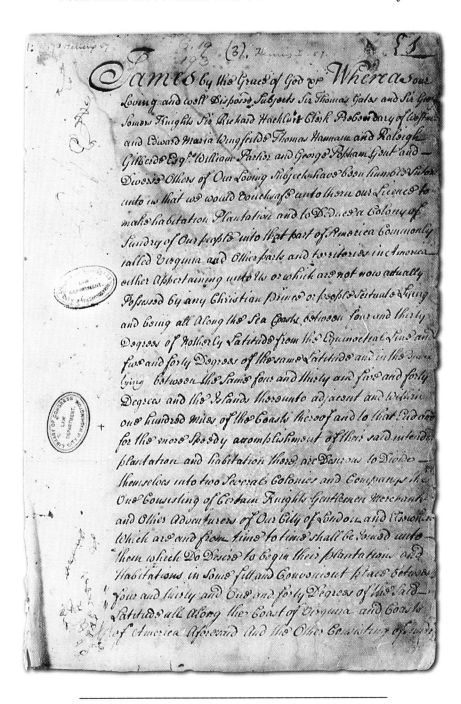

The April 10, 1606, Charter of Virginia outlined the geographic boundaries and the conditions whereby King James I granted permission for a group of businessmen to establish an English colony in "that part of America commonly called VIRGINIA."

civilized society. The English believed the Indians lived as savages, and hoped to help them live properly by converting them to Christianity.

The colonists spent the first two weeks in Virginia sailing around the area searching for a site to set up their colony. On April 27, 1607, a small group left the ship to explore on land. After a few days, the Englishmen spotted five Powhatan Indians on the shore and greeted the Indians with a sign of friendship, a hand over the heart. The Indians responded in a friendly manner and invited the Englishmen to their town, Kecoughtan. The newcomers were treated as guests. As was the custom among the Powhatans, the colonists were invited to feast with the Powhatans. The Powhatans entertained the colonists with dancing. The Indians also offered the English a pipe of tobacco, which symbolized intentions of peace between the Powhatans and the settlers.

As the English continued to explore, they came in contact with various Powhatan groups. The encounters were generally friendly. As they had been in Kecoughtan, the English were invited into the Indian towns and treated as honored guests. In return the English gave the Native Americans gifts of glass

Next spread: John Smith's 1607 exploration of the coastal waters, terrain, and population of Virginia was the groundwork for his 1608 map of Virginia. Smith's map was engraved and printed in a number of publications. William Hole's engraving of the map was published in London, England, in 1624.

37°

38

MONACANS

MANN

POWHATAN
Held this state & fashion when Capt. Smith
was deliuered to him prisoner
1607

MAN-
GOAGS

CHE-
WONS

P

O

W

H

A

T

Monahassanugh
Rassawek
Monasukapanough

Massinacack

Mowhemcho

Massawomeck

The Fales
Powhatan
Orapaks
Cattachiptico
Passaunkack

Arrohatteck

Appamattuck

Nechanico
Shockhonk
Attamuck
Poctanco
Accossiwinck
Kapknock
Weyanoke
Menapacunt
Quiyoughcohanock
Mattaponient
Manamahkemanck
Menanhaunt
Pasaughtacock
Poruptanck
Matchut

Onackeckowan
Myghtuckpassun
Ayocant
Utcustank
Accoqueck
Secobeck
Martoughquaunk
Anaskenoans
Muttamussinsack
Nandtaughtacund
Aurenapeugh
Checopissowo
Assuwesho
Papiscone
Kerabeak
Pissasec
Nawacaten

James
Towne

Mattcock
Werowcomoco

Opiscopanck
Cantaunkack
Capahowasick
Warraskoyack

Warrankatank

Kecoughtan
Nandtaughtacund
Menaskunt
Anthenb
Werowocomoco
Nepatawun
Opiscatumeck
Kapawnu
Cekakawwon
Cuttatawoman
Cekakawwon
Onaumanient
Nomini
Matchopick
Secacawoni

SEA

Wavratborack
Mokete

Nandsamund
Mattanock
Teracosick
Skicoac
Manchoughquemec
Chesapeack
Mortons baye

Ceder Ile
Cossiold Ile
Tindals poynt
Tyffins poynt
Poynt Warde
Point comfort

CH:

Russels Iles

Accohanock
Keales In
Accomuck
Keales poynt
Wighcocomoco

Mathees poynt
Nause

KVSKA

Cape Henry

Cape Charle

Smyths Iles

THE

VIRGINIAN

SEA

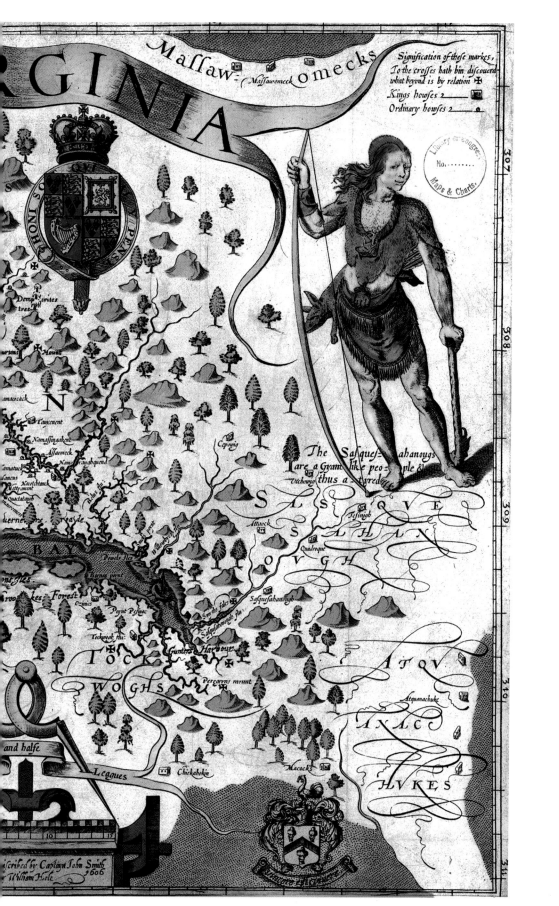

These glass beads were uncovered during modern excavation of the James Fort at Jamestown. Beads of this type were made in the Venetian Republic in the 1500s and 1600s. The colonists were supplied with trading beads such as these before they departed Europe for North America.

beads, bells, needles, and pins. These objects were interesting to the Powhatans, who graciously accepted them.

Finally, in May, the settlers came across an island in the James River. They found the island a suitable place to build their colony and named it James Island. There were no Indians living on the island. The land could be easily defended against enemy attacks, as it was surrounded by deep water. The depth of the water also allowed the colonists to anchor their ships close to shore. There were, however, two things that would mar the seeming perfection of the spot. Nearby was a swamp that bred mosquitoes. In addition, the colonists did not know that in the summer the fresh water of the James River would turn brackish and undrinkable.

4. Culture Conflict

The English colonists and the Indians continued to trade with one another. In addition to bringing novelties such as beads and bells, the English also brought metal axes and knives, which the Powhatans considered useful and valuable. The Powhatans gave the English furs and much-needed food.

The Powhatans were curious about the newcomers. The Powhatans wondered if the English would make good allies against rival Indian groups or if the English would prove to be foes. Before the colonists settled on James Island in May, the Powhatans had mistaken the English for visitors and not for people who intended to remain on Powhatan land. One of the reasons for this mistaken idea might have been that the English did not bring any women with them when they first arrived. The Powhatans assumed the English were not staying because their families were not with them.

Immediately after their arrival at James Island, the English began to build their colony, which included a fort. On the first night, some Powhatans from the town

The modern artist Sidney King depicted John Smith trading with Native Americans. Jamestown colonists were eager to trade for corn, but corn harvests were not always plentiful in Virginia. The Powhatans were sometimes unable or unwilling to satisfy English demand for this crop.

of Paspahegh came paddling around the settlement at around midnight. They had come to investigate the construction of the fort. The fort suggested that the English would remain on the island and that they were concerned about defending themselves. Sir George Percy, one of the colonists, wrote in an essay from about 1606 that some Powhatans came near but then ran away when another colonist noticed them and sounded an alarm.

During this early period of the Jamestown Colony, there were occasions when the English and Powhatan cultures clashed. The Native Americans and the

Europeans often misunderstood one another's actions. For example, a few days after the Indians had first come to investigate the construction of the fort, the weroance of Paspahegh and about one hundred Powhatan men paid a visit to Jamestown. The weroance, whose name was Wowinchopunck, had already met the English. Two weeks before, Wowinchopunck had welcomed some of the colonists into his town as guests. When he visited Jamestown, Wowinchopunck brought a gift of food and a deer. He made gestures that indicated he was willing to give the English more land on which to settle.

The visit seemed to be going well until one of the Powhatans took a hatchet that belonged to a colonist. The Englishman seized his hatchet back and struck the Powhatan. Another Powhatan went to the aid of the man who had been struck. In response to this scuffle, the English took up their weapons. At the sight of the armed colonists, the Indians became angry and left.

The colonists regarded the taking of the hatchet as a theft. In the months to come, the colonists would often accuse the Indians of stealing from them. Gabriel Archer, one of the colonists, described in an essay from around 1607, "The people steal any thing [that] comes neare them, yea are so practiced in this art that lookeng in our face they would with their foot betwene their toes convey a chizell, knife . . . or any indifferent light thing."

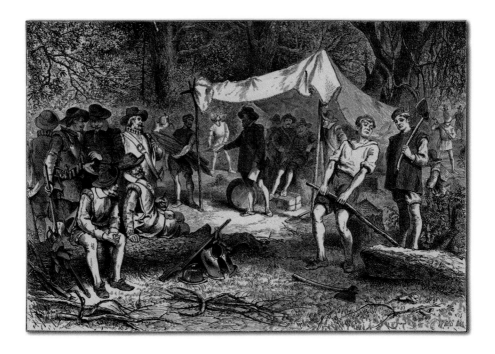

Many of Jamestown's first settlers came to Virginia hoping to become rich. There were rumors that gold and pearls were plentiful in America. The British poet Michael Drayton's 1606 "Ode to the Virginian Voyage" fueled such dreams by naming Virginia "Earth's only paradise!" This engraving of the Jamestown colonists was published in 1876.

For the Powhatan Indians, however, taking something from the English was not considered a wrongful act. In Powhatan culture, it was only wrong to steal from other Powhatans. Stealing from outsiders was allowed.

In addition, the English perceived fair trade as bartering one object for another, in an exchange that both parties had agreed upon. The Indians, however, did not have this concept. The Powhatans' conception of trade was an exchange of gifts between parties. One side would offer gifts without expecting anything in return at the time the gifts were given. The Powhatan would, however, expect to be given gifts in return at a later date. Therefore, whenever the Powhatans entertained the English with lavish feasts and gifts of food, and the English did not return their generosity at a later time in equally generous ways, the Indians felt they had a right to take what they wanted from the English. The Powhatan who took the hatchet was probably taking what he felt was a fair gift because the English had been well feasted in his town two weeks earlier.

The concept of authority was another source of misunderstanding between the English and the Powhatans. The Powhatan weroances commanded great respect and loyalty from the people they ruled, so the English assumed that the weroances had complete control over their people. This was not always the case. Therefore, when a weroance made peace with the English and some of his people continued to show hostility, the English assumed that the chief was treacherous or dishonest. In reality, the chiefs, including Chief Powhatan, did not always have the power to make their people obey them.

Language was a barrier between the English and the Powhatans as well. During their initial encounters, the English and the Powhatans communicated mostly through gestures. Captain John Smith, a leader of the Jamestown Colony, dealt frequently with the Indians, so it was necessary for him to learn some of the

Listed here are some of the Powhatan words that John Smith included in his 1612 book, A Map of Virginia. *The English words are spelled the way John Smith recorded them in his book.*

Nemarough	A man
Crenepo	A woman
Marowanchesso	A boy
Yehawkans	Houses
Mockasins	Shooes
Tussan	Beds
Pokatawer	Fire
Attawp	A bowe
Attonce	Arrowes
Tomahacks	Axes
Pamesacks	Knives
Suckahanna	Water
Noughmass	Fish
Netoppew	Friends
Marrapough	Enimies

Algonquian languages.

Pocahontas helped John Smith to learn her language. During their meetings, which probably took place at Jamestown, Pocahontas taught Smith Native American words such as *tomahacks*, an Algonquian word for axes, and *pawcussacks*, a word for guns. The instruction was not one-sided, however. Pocahontas began to learn English vocabulary from Smith. As Smith's knowledge progressed, he translated useful sentences to further his trade with the Powhatans. Smith wrote in his book

The title page from Captain John Smith's 1624 *The Generall Historie of Virginia, New-England, and the Summer Isles*. The "Summer Isles" refers to the islands of Bermuda.

Generall Historie that he translated the following sentence into Algonquian, "Bid Pokahuntas bring hither two little Baskets, and I will give her white Beads to make her a chaine."

In his book *A Map of Virginia*, written in 1612, Smith included a list of Powhatan words, numbers, and phrases. The colonist William Strachey also compiled a book, *A Dictionarie of the Indian Language*. In the fall of 1609, Smith sent a boy named Henry Spelman to live with the Powhatans. Spelman was probably about twelve years old at the time and he learned Algonquian during his stay with the Powhatans. This knowledge allowed Spelman to become the colony's best interpreter.

In time the cultural differences between the Powhatans and the English would cause bitterness. The English did not think they were doing anything wrong, and the Indians found the English increasingly rude and offensive.

5. The Struggle to Survive in Jamestown

In June 1607, Captain Christopher Newport, who had commanded the three ships that had brought the colonists to Virginia, returned to England with two of the ships. He left the colonists with enough supplies to last until September and promised to return from England with more. At around the same time, Powhatan sent word to the newcomers by way of a messenger. The messenger told the colonists that Powhatan wanted to have a peaceful relationship with them and that Powhatan had told his people to allow the settlers to grow their own crops without being disturbed. In addition, the Indians brought the colonists gifts of food throughout the summer. Pocahontas, in the company of other Indians, came to Jamestown with baskets of corn. She told Smith which Indian groups in the region might be open to trading with the English.

The colonists, however, did not conserve their store of supplies and soon ran out of food. They did not have the skills to produce their own food, nor did they intend to learn how to produce their own food. The Virginia

Company had instructed them to find riches in this new place and to use the region's natural resources to create goods that could be exported to England. Colonists were not expected to spend their days growing food. Instead, they were expected to use the supplies they arrived with and to get whatever additional food they needed by trading with the local Indian groups.

The settlers of Jamestown were gentlemen, not farmers. The settlers were also unfamiliar with the new environment and did not know how to hunt and track animals as the Native American men did. They did not know how to find plants that were safe and nutritious to eat. The Jamestown colonists began to starve and became ill from diseases such as typhoid and dysentery, which were caused by drinking the brackish water of the James River. Some colonists ran away to live with the Indians. By November 1607, the colony that had originated with 104 people had been reduced to only 40 people.

In September 1607, as the colonists were dying, Captain John Smith took action to save them. The third ship that had brought the colonists across the Atlantic Ocean was still in the colony. Smith used the ship to go in search of corn. He would trade European goods to acquire grain from the Indians.

John Smith, who was twenty-seven years old in 1607, proved himself a capable and an energetic leader in the early days of the colony. Smith was a mercenary who had traveled the world and had

Captain John Smith, shown in a portrait from around 1616, was frustrated by Jamestown's gentleman colonists who were often lazy or unwilling to work. After Smith became president of the colony in 1608, he declared that "He that will not work shall not eat."

earned a reputation as a courageous soldier. Unlike the other colonists, Smith was a yeoman, or farmer, not a gentleman. He saw the New World as an opportunity to improve his social standing.

Smith and the English stopped first at Kecoughtan, the town where the colonists had been so warmly welcomed with feasting the previous April. This time, however, the people of Kecoughtan were not as friendly. They did not invite the English into their town and demanded weapons in exchange for a small amount of corn.

The next day the Indians did invite the English into their town, but by then Smith had grown suspicious. As they entered the town, Smith ordered his men to fire four shots as a warning to the Indians. The settlers were armed and would defend themselves if necessary. There was no feasting and no gift giving. Instead, the two sides traded in the European tradition and made deals that seemed fair to both.

During one of their trading expeditions in December 1607, Smith and his companions were attacked by a large party of Indian hunters led by Powhatan's brother Opechancanough. Smith's companions were killed and he was taken prisoner. The hunters took him to a camp called Rasawrack, where they held Smith until the hunt was over.

Smith was treated well while in captivity. He was allowed to send a message to Jamestown explaining what had happened, and he was well fed. According to

Jacob de Gheyn's 1608 engraving of a soldier illustrated *The Exercise of Armes*, a military training manual that instructed soldiers in the use of weapons such as the musket. Although the manual was published in Amsterdam, the Jamestown colonists were similarly outfitted to defend themselves.

Smith, who documented his experience in the 1624 *Generall Historie*, each morning he was given "three great platters of fine bread, more venison than ten men could devour." Priests also examined Smith to see if he was dangerous. The priests performed a ritual and declared him harmless.

In the weeks following the hunt, Opechancanough traveled with Smith to other Powhatan towns, where Smith was received as a guest. On one of these stops, Smith was taken to a place situated along the Rappahannock River. The year before, a European ship had arrived in the area and the ship's captain had killed the local weroance and kidnapped some Powhatans. Smith was brought to the area so that the Indians could see if Smith was that same captain. The Indians saw that Smith was not the same person and declared him to be innocent. Finally, Opechancanough brought Smith to the town of Werowocomoco on the York River, where Chief Powhatan lived.

In the seven months that the colonists had been in Jamestown, Powhatan had never attempted to meet them. Captain John Smith was the first colonist to meet the paramount.

6. Did Pocahontas Rescue John Smith?

Powhatan welcomed Captain John Smith at Werowocomoco. Smith later described the chief as "a tall well proportioned man . . . his head somwhat gray, his beard so thinne that it seemeth none at al. His age neare 60; of a very able and hardy body to endure any labour."

Despite the language barrier, the two men communicated as best they could. Powhatan asked why the English had come. Smith was not truthful in his answer. He replied that the Spanish had damaged their ships and that the Jamestown colonists were planning to stay only until Captain Newport returned to take them back to England. Powhatan seemed contented with the answer and told Smith that the Indians would give the English food if they would make iron tools and copper ornaments for him in return. Powhatan also encouraged Smith to settle in an area close to Powhatan and offered to give Smith some land for that purpose. Powhatan then sent Smith back to Jamestown.

This was the account that Smith described in *True Relation*, written in 1608. In 1624, however, Smith wrote an additional account of this event that has become an American legend. Smith claimed that Powhatan sentenced him to death. Smith was dragged to a large stone and forced to lay his head on it as Powhatan's men prepared to smash his head with a club. According to this story, Pocahontas saved Smith's life when she placed her own head over Smith's to stop the execution. Smith always wrote about himself as if he was talking about another person. He reported, "Pocahontas the Kings dearest daughter . . . got his head in her armes, and laid her owne upon his to save him from death: whereat the Emperour was contented he should live."

Some contemporary scholars think this event never happened. In his earlier writings about his capture, Smith never mentioned anything about Powhatan sentencing him to death. He did not write about Pocahontas saving him. In 1624, seventeen years later, Smith included these details. Why would Smith leave out such an important event in the first account of his capture? Furthermore, none of the other colonists documented this story. Such a dramatic event would certainly have made it into the Jamestown records before seventeen years had passed.

Smith was an energetic and enterprising leader, but he was also proud and boastful. In his writings about

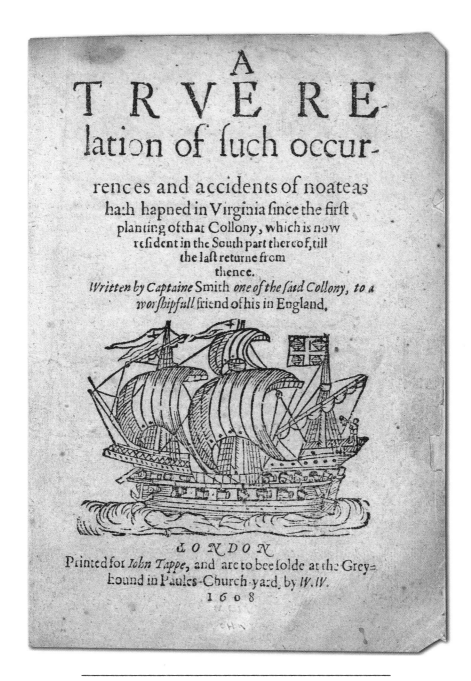

This is the title page from John Smith's 1608 *A True Relation of such occurrences and accidents of noate as hath hapned in Virginia since the first planting of that Collony, which is now resident in the South part thereof, till the last returne from thence*. Smith was initially unaware that this account of his life in Virginia had been sent to a London publisher.

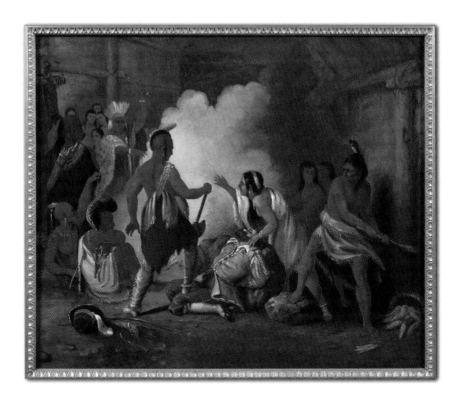

Pocahontas Saving the Life of Captain John Smith was created by John Gadsby Chapman around 1836. Smith's contemporaries did not question the truth of Smith's 1624 account of his rescue. Not until the 1860s did historians begin to debate the accuracy of Smith's story. History is often revised, as historians can only make their analyses from the information that is available to them at the time of their research.

his world travels and adventures, he often described himself as a hero. His written accounts describe how on three different occasions, a young woman saved his life.

Some historians doubt that Smith's life was ever in danger. Clubbing was a death the Powhatans reserved for criminals and for those who were disobedient to their chiefs. It was not the Powhatan custom to execute foreigners except during battle. Also, Chief Powhatan had already consulted his priests, who had said Smith was not a threat. The advice of priests was taken seriously, so it is unlikely that Powhatan would not have trusted them. If Smith presented no threat to Powhatan and his people, then there was no reason to kill him.

Other modern scholars think that if the event did happen as Smith described, it was not a life-threatening event. The description of what happened after Pocahontas rescued Smith sounds like it might have been part of a ceremonial adoption ritual. Smith said that after his rescue he was taken to a house in the woods where Powhatan and some of his men had been painted black. Smith wrote that they made a "most dolefullest noyse [sorrowful noise]" in another room and then came to Smith and announced that they were friends. Powhatan also declared Smith the ruler of Capahosic, one of Powhatan's towns. The chief also said Smith was now his son. In many Native American cultures, it was the custom to have ceremonies in which a captive would be adopted into a particular family. However, if this was an adoption ritual, Smith was not aware of it, and neither he nor any of the other Jamestown colonists ever wrote about this being such a ceremony.

Some historians offer a third interpretation. They say that Chief Powhatan might have been testing Smith's courage by threatening his life. The Powhatans greatly respected and admired bravery. Powhatan men were trained from boyhood to value courage. They were taught to hide fear and to die bravely in battle.

However, some historians believe that the story is true and that Smith chose not to write about it while he was still in Jamestown. He might have been embarrassed to let his fellow colonists know that a young girl had saved his life.

The story of Pocahontas's rescue of John Smith's life may be false. On the other hand, the story may be true, or it may even be an exaggerated account of something that did occur. Historians will probably never know for sure.

7. Rising Tensions

Captain John Smith returned to Jamestown in January 1608 to find that Captain Newport had arrived from England with fresh supplies for the colony and about one hundred new settlers. However, within one week of Smith's return, a fire broke out in Jamestown that destroyed the colonist's homes, clothing, and most of the food supply. The colonists were once again in need of aid. Powhatan, seeing that the English required help, began to send them food on a regular basis. Smith wrote that the food included "bread, fish, turkies, squirrels, deare and other wild beasts" and was usually delivered by Pocahontas.

Smith's pleasure in Pocahontas's visits was obvious to others. Several Jamestown colonists who later documented their experiences in a 1612 account stated that "Very oft [Pocahontas] came to our fort, with what she could get for Captaine Smith. . . . Her especially he ever much respected."

In exchange for the food that Powhatan sent to Jamestown, Captain Newport sent gifts to Powhatan. The chief continued to ask Newport and Smith to come and visit him. Finally, in late February 1608, the two men visited Powhatan, accompanied by a group of the Jamestown colonists.

John Smith gave Powhatan presents, which included a white dog, a red coat, and a hat. Smith also promised to be an ally to Powhatan against Powhatan's enemies. The colonists were given gifts of bread. Smith reminded Powhatan that he had offered to give Smith some land close to where Powhatan lived. Chief Powhatan said he would offer the land, but first the English had to agree to live under Powhatan's rule. Smith did not agree to that.

The visit between the colonists and Powhatan lasted several days. During this visit, Newport gave the care of an English boy named Thomas Savage over to Powhatan and his people. This act was intended to be a sign of the colonists' goodwill, as the English were entrusting one of their own children to Powhatan. The English also had another motive for doing this. They sent Thomas to live with the Indians so that he could learn their language and become an interpreter. Powhatan later gave an Indian boy named Namontack to the English for the same reason.

Although the visit was peaceful, Powhatan and Smith were cautious of each other. Each began to realize that the other man wanted the upper hand in trade negotiations. Neither man was willing to surrender his own will to the other. For example, early in 1608, Powhatan had sent Newport twenty turkeys

This replica of a late-1500s basket-hilt broadsword typifies the type of sword that was used by the Jamestown colonists. The sturdy broadsword was an all-purpose weapon. Broadsword remains have been discovered at Jamestown and in the Chesapeake Bay area. The English traded their broadswords to obtain food from the Indians.

and some corn, and had asked for twenty swords in exchange. Newport accepted the turkeys and sent the swords to Powhatan. Later, Powhatan sent turkeys to Smith and again requested that swords be sent in return. Smith did not send the weapons. Smith's decision insulted Powhatan and increased the tension between the two men.

On April 10, 1608, Newport left for England to obtain more supplies for the colonists. He took Namontack with him. In England the Native American boy was introduced by the Virginia Company as a son of "the emperor of Virginia."

That spring of 1608, the Jamestown colonists began having military drills outside their fort. The men were preparing to explore the land along the James River, beyond the falls. After observing the drills, the Powhatans became suspicious. They believed the men were preparing for an attack against them. Chief Powhatan sent Thomas Savage back to Jamestown to find out what the men were doing and instructed Thomas to ask the colonists if they were planning an attack on the Powhatans.

The colonists replied that they intended to go to Powhatan's town "to seeke stones to make Hatchets." This was a poor excuse. The colonists had metal hatchets and therefore had no need for stones to make their tools. Powhatan was so insulted by the lie that he gave his people permission to pester the English and to take tools from their fort. This behavior became so common that in time the colonists took Native American hostages in order to get the tools back. To get even, the Indians took two English hostages. The English then raided and burned some Powhatan towns in revenge. Although the Indians then released the English prisoners, the English released only one of the Indian captives.

Finally, Powhatan and his brother Opechancanough sent messages to the colonists asking that they set the Indian prisoners free. The person who brought Powhatan's message was Pocahontas.

Pocahontas arrived at the fort and delivered her father's request and a gift of corn. An Indian man by the name of Rawhunt accompanied her. Rawhunt explained to the colonists that Powhatan was showing faith in the English by sending his daughter to them. Pocahontas avoided looking at the Indian prisoners. Powhatan warriors were proud and being held in captivity must have been shameful to them. Pocahontas took care not to embarrass the hostages further by glancing at them. Later that same day, some of the prisoners' friends and relatives came to the fort, accompanied by a messenger from Opechancanough. The messenger asked that the captives be freed. Smith released the prisoners to Pocahontas.

The colonists continued to explore the area throughout the summer of 1608, trading with the Indian groups they encountered as they traveled farther away from the center of Powhatan's domain. In September 1608, John Smith was elected president of the Jamestown Colony. He was the colony's third president and had been preceded in the position by Edward Maria Wingfield and Captain John Ratcliffe. In October, Newport arrived with supplies and more colonists, including the colony's first women. He also brought gifts for Powhatan from King James, such as a bed, some English clothes, and a crown.

In England, Newport had been given instructions to crown Powhatan. The English hoped that the gifts and the crowning would please the chief and make him more willing to continue trading with the colonists. However, as Powhatan refused to go to Jamestown to collect his gifts, Smith and his men went to Powhatan's capital, Werowocomoco instead.

The night before the colonists met with the chief in Werowocomoco, some Powhatans led Smith and his party to a field and seated the men on mats that had been set around a fire. When cries and shouts were heard from the darkness, Smith and his men feared they had been set up for an attack and prepared to defend themselves. They grabbed their guns and took some Powhatans as hostages. Pocahontas saw their reaction and promised the English that they were in no danger.

King James I, who was painted by Paul van Somer around 1610, did not promote religious freedom in Virginia. The colony's leaders took an oath vowing to defend the king against the pope and the Catholic Church.

The men were then treated to a ritualistic dance. Thirty women costumed as warriors danced and sang for an hour. Pocahontas had arranged this entertainment on behalf of the English visitors.

The next day Powhatan was not pleased with the coronation. He was annoyed that the English were trying to put a crown on his head and he refused to kneel. The English finally were able to crown Powhatan by pushing on his shoulders and slipping the crown onto his head as he stooped.

In the fall and the winter of 1608, the colonists found that few Indians were willing to trade corn with them. Meanwhile, Newport left Virginia for a third time to get more supplies for the colonists, who were dangerously low on food. Not until the spring of 1609 did the Virginia Company agree to send more supplies.

By January 1609, Smith realized that the situation at Jamestown was desperate. Once again the colonists were starving, but this time, unlike the last, Pocahontas was not being sent by her father to bring gifts of food to Jamestown. Smith planned to obtain food by force and he contemplated launching a surprise attack on Powhatan at Werowocomoco. As he was considering this plan, Powhatan made Smith an offer. Smith could have corn if he would send men to build an English-style house for Powhatan and if he would give the chief additional gifts, including swords and muskets. Powhatan realized that he was expecting a great deal from Smith, but he knew the colonists were desperate for food. Smith agreed to the trade and sent some men to begin work on the house. Smith did not, however, send Powhatan the weapons.

Smith and his men arrived at Werowocomoco on January 12, 1609. Powhatan offered the men a feast, and the Indians and the colonists began to trade. During the visit, Powhatan warned Smith that the settlers should not attempt to control Powhatan or to seize his lands. Powhatan said the starving colonists were in no condition to fight and could not defeat the Indians. The chief also warned Smith that the Indians could move out of reach of the English and could leave the colonists behind to starve. Smith argued that the colonists were not as dependent on the Indians as Powhatan thought.

As the trade negotiations continued, the two men disputed over the worth of what they were trading. Smith felt Powhatan was not offering enough corn for what Powhatan was getting in return. Powhatan remained firm in his demand for weapons.

Powhatan tried to reason with Smith and pointed out that the colonists needed corn that only the Indians could provide. The chief also realized that the English were so desperate for food that they might attack his people and take the corn by force. Powhatan knew how effective the English weapons were against the Native American bows and arrows and war clubs. Smith, on the other hand, recognized that if he continued to supply Powhatan with weapons through trade, he would be putting his own people in danger.

Powhatan, in a speech to Smith, explained that he preferred to have a friendly relationship with the English colonists. Powhatan reasoned, ". . . it is better to eate good meate, lie well, and sleepe quietly . . . laugh and be merry with you, have copper, hatchets, or what I want being your friend; then be forced to flie from al, to lie in cold woods, feed upon acorns, roots, and such trash, and be so hunted by you, that I can neither rest, eat, nor sleepe."

At this point, however, negotiations faltered as there was too much distrust between Powhatan and Smith. Smith knew that he could not give any more weapons to the Indians. The Powhatans already outnumbered the English, and having muskets and swords was the colonists' only advantage. Powhatan, however, demanded weapons in trade. If Smith would agree to trade food for weapons, it would be proof that Smith was committed to peace.

Both men had come to the meeting prepared to attack the other if peace could not be established. At some point in this meeting, Powhatan slipped out of the village with most of the women and children. The chief left only a few women behind to keep Smith from suspecting that anything was afoot. Powhatan's men then quietly encircled Smith's quarters but were spotted by the English. The English suspected that the Powhatans had surrounded them in preparation for an attack and quickly picked up their weapons. The Indians retreated.

Shortly after this occurred, Powhatan sent Smith a gift with a message saying that the English had misunderstood the Indians' behavior. Smith did not believe this explanation.

Smith's suspicions were correct. Pocahontas came to his quarters that night to warn him that her father intended to kill Smith and his men. Smith wrote in his *Generall Historie* that Pocahontas urged him that ". . . if we [wanted to] live shee wished us presently to be gone." In appreciation of her warning, Smith offered Pocahontas a small token, possibly in the form of beads. The gesture made Pocahontas cry. She refused the gift. If she were caught with such a present it would alert her father to her treason, "for if Powhatan should know it, she were but dead." Smith wrote that "shee ranne away by herselfe as she came."

Smith and his men left the town. After this incident, Powhatan moved his residence to the town of Orapax, farther from the English, where he felt safer.

8. Pocahontas Is Kidnapped

Because Powhatan and John Smith were unable to come to an agreement, the hostilities between the Indians and the colonists continued. Smith persisted in intimidating the local groups into giving him corn, and Powhatan attempted to have Smith killed. On one occasion, Smith survived being poisoned while on a visit to an Indian town.

Throughout these periods of violence, Pocahontas tried to help the English whenever she could. In 1609, not long after Smith and his party had departed Werowocomoco, the colonist Richard Wiffin went searching for Smith at Werowocomoco. Wiffin's mission was to inform Smith of a disaster at Jamestown. A boat had overturned on the James River and a number of colonists had drowned.

Pocahontas found Wiffin and offered him shelter and a hiding place before sending him in the direction of Pamunkey, where Smith and his men had traveled in search of corn. Powhatan warriors soon learned that a colonist was in the area. They began to search for him.

To prevent Wiffin's capture, Pocahontas sent the warriors in the wrong direction to find him.

At the time of the spring planting in 1609, the Powhatans sought another truce with the English. By the summer, however, violence had again erupted between the English and the Powhatans.

After a bad harvest, the colonists were increasingly discontented with John Smith's leadership. In September, just as his term as president was coming to an end, Smith was badly burned in an accident when some gunpowder exploded. No longer wanted as leader, and in great pain, John Smith left the Jamestown Colony on October 4, 1609, and sailed back to England. He never returned to Virginia. Smith did not say good-bye to his friend Pocahontas.

When Pocahontas returned to Jamestown after Smith had left, the colonists told her that Smith was dead. Perhaps the colonists assumed Smith would not survive his injury, or perhaps they wanted to spare her feelings because Smith had not said good-bye. After Smith's departure, Pocahontas chose to cease her visits to Jamestown.

In 1609, King James I granted a second charter to the Virginia Company. By this time it was clear that there was no gold in Virginia. There was no northwest passage in Virginia that led to Asia. The Virginia Company assigned the colony a different goal. Jamestown was to become a place of industry, producing goods that could

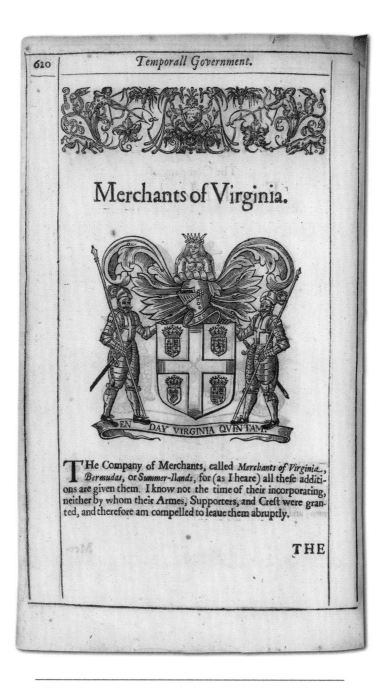

620   *Temporall Government.*

Merchants of Virginia.

EN DAY VIRGINIA QVINTAM.

THe Company of Merchants, called *Merchants of Virginia*, *Bermudas*, or *Summer-Ilands*, for (as I heare) all these additions are given them. I know not the time of their incorporating, neither by whom their Armes, Supporters, and Crest were granted, and therefore am compelled to leaue them abruptly.

THE

Shown above is a 1633 engraving of the Virginia Company's coat of arms. A coat of arms was initially a piece of decorated cloth that was draped over a medieval soldier's armor to protect him from the sun and to identify him should he be killed in battle. Later a coat of arms became an emblem that identified families, property, and businesses.

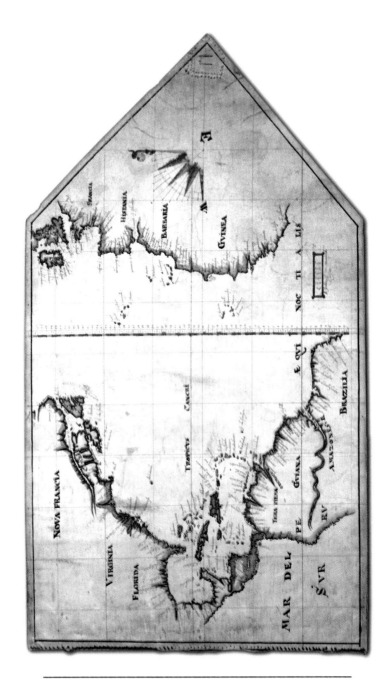

The Virginia Company of London created this Virginia Chart around 1607. The chart was probably designed to promote the settlement of Virginia. To place the New World in perspective for Europeans, the map depicted the western shores of Europe and Africa at the top of the page and the New World coastline, which included Virginia, at the bottom.

be exported to England, such as clapboard, a building material made of wood. However, the most successful industry proved to be the cultivation of tobacco, which was a cash crop that became the main export from Jamestown. The colonists were also expected to grow enough food to support themselves.

The winter of 1609–1610, however, proved to be a time of intense struggle for the colonists. The small amount of rainfall that had fallen in 1609 meant the Powhatans did not have much corn for themselves, let alone a surplus, or excess, of corn to trade with the colonists.

During this difficult period, Powhatan invited the English captain John Ratcliffe to trade at Orapax, where the chief was then living. When Ratcliffe arrived, he and his men were ambushed and killed by the Indians. Only one of Ratcliffe's men escaped, out of an assembled group of thirty or forty men.

Henry Spelman and Thomas Savage, the English boys sent to live with Powhatan, also managed to flee during this time. Both Henry and Thomas still had been living with the chief during this period of hostility. Anxious for their safety, Henry, Thomas, and another English boy, Samuel, fled from Orapax but were overtaken by some Powhatan warriors. Samuel was killed and Thomas Savage chose to return to Chief Powhatan. Henry Spelman escaped the warriors with the help of Pocahontas. He fled from Orapax and went to live at Patawomeck, where, according to John Smith, who later wrote about this event in England, Henry Spelman "lived many yeeres after, by [Pocahontas's] meanes." Spelman also discussed the escape in an account called *The Relation of Virginea*.

The colonists continued to endure terrible suffering in what they would come to call the Starving Time. Desperate for food, the settlers ate dogs, cats, rats, snakes, and, in some cases, the bodies of people who had died. John Smith wrote about the Starving Time in the *Generall Historie of Virginia*. He described how ". . . of five hundred [colonists] within six moneths after Captaine Smiths departure, there remained not past sixtie men, women, and children, most miserable and poore creatures; and those were preserved for the most part by roots, herbes, acornes, walnuts, berries, now and than a little fish: they that had starch in these extremities made no small use of it; yea, even the very skinnes of our horses [were eaten]."

The Starving Time, which lasted from the fall of 1609 to the spring of 1610, also marked the beginning of a period of intense warfare between the English and the Indians that was to last until 1614. Some scholars call this the First Anglo-Powhatan War.

In May 1610, two English ships, commanded by Sir Thomas Gates and Sir George Sommers, arrived in Virginia bringing fresh provisions and additional colonists. Gates was horrified by the conditions he found in Jamestown and decided to evacuate the

The Jamestown colonists carry out their dead for burial during the Starving Time. During the winter of 1609 to 1610, about 80 percent of the colonists died. One potential source of food that the Jamestown colonists overlooked were crabs from the Chesapeake Bay.

colony and bring all the colonists back to England.

The colonists were overjoyed to leave their misery behind and sail for home. However, on the second day of the voyage, the ships met another ship on its way to Jamestown. This ship was one of a fleet that had been under the command of Thomas West, who was known as Lord De La Warr. The fleet had been scheduled to bring supplies to the colony the year before but had been delayed by a hurricane. This ship carried three hundred additional colonists and plenty of provisions. The departing ships turned around and the colonists returned to

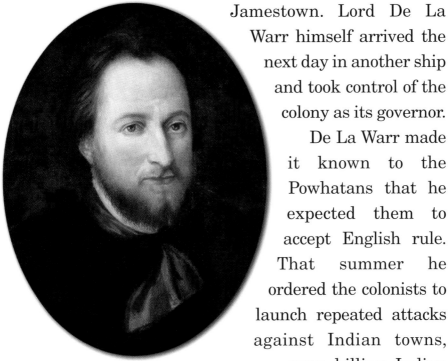

Margaret Thomas based her 1882 portrait of Lord De La Warr on a painting done by Wybrand Simonsz de Geest in the 1600s. Both the Delaware River and the U.S. state Delaware were named after Lord De La Warr.

Jamestown. Lord De La Warr himself arrived the next day in another ship and took control of the colony as its governor.

De La Warr made it known to the Powhatans that he expected them to accept English rule. That summer he ordered the colonists to launch repeated attacks against Indian towns, even killing Indian women and children. The English also burned the Indians' homes and fields. In July, De La Warr sent a message to Powhatan asking if the chief wanted peace or war. Peace would require the Indians to return English captives and stolen goods. Powhatan did not agree to the terms of peace. He responded by telling De La Warr that the English should get out of Virginia. De La Warr continued his attacks on the Indians.

In one of the English attacks on the Indian town of Paspahegh, a wife of the weroance and her two children were taken captive. The English then shot the children and later killed the mother. In Powhatan culture, women and children were never killed in warfare. This incident so outraged the Powhatans that they started to launch attacks of their own. Both the English and the Indians were engaged in brutal war. There was no more talk of peace.

As the winter of 1610 approached, the colonists did not starve as they had in previous years. They had plenty of provisions and were well organized under De La Warr's leadership. In March 1611, De La Warr returned to England because of illness and was replaced temporarily by Sir Thomas Dale. Dale was an efficient leader who kept the colony running well until August, when Sir Thomas Gates assumed command. Meanwhile, as the First Anglo-Powhatan War waged, the English expanded their colony. After Gates took control, Dale and a party of men went looking for new areas to build settlements. Dale went upriver with 350 colonists and began building a new settlement, which they named Henrico.

During this period, the colonists did manage to trade with a few Indian groups. One of these groups was the Patawomeck, with whom the English admiral Samuel Argall of Jamestown had made peace in December 1612. The following April, in 1613, Argall learned that Pocahontas, then a young woman of about eighteen, was visiting the Patawomecks. She had come for a stay

This 1619 engraving by Theodore de Bry, based on a work by Georg Keller, depicts several events. On the left Iopassus and his wife persuade Pocahontas to come aboard an English ship. On the right Pocahontas is taken to the ship where she will be held hostage.

of about three months, both to visit with friends and to trade on behalf of her father with the Indians of that town. When Argall heard this news, he devised a plan to kidnap Pocahontas and hold her hostage until her father would agree to return all the English captives and the stolen tools and weapons.

Argall went to the Patawomecks and asked the weroance Iopassus to help him. He assured Iopassus that if Powhatan became angry with the Patawomecks because of Iopassus's involvement in the kidnapping, the English would protect him and his people. If Iopassus refused to help the English, then the peace between them would cease. If he cooperated, the English promised to give Iopassus a copper kettle.

The plot to kidnap Pocahontas involved one of Iopassus's wives. The woman pretended that she wanted to see Argall's ship and she persuaded Pocahontas to go along with her. The two women and Iopassus spent the night on board the ship, and Pocahontas was given a private room. The next day she was not allowed to leave the ship. Although she was unhappy, Pocahontas's reaction to her captivity was to accept it quietly.

9. Pocahontas and John Rolfe

Admiral Samuel Argall sent a message to Chief Powhatan that his daughter had been kidnapped and taken to Jamestown. Argall told Powhatan what he wanted in return for Pocahontas, and Powhatan agreed. The chief sent some English captives and some tools and weapons as partial payment for his daughter's release. Powhatan also included a message with the ransom, saying that he would send a gift of corn after Pocahontas was returned to him and that peace would be restored. The English, however, refused to send Pocahontas back to her father until all their captives and property had been returned to them. As a result, Pocahontas remained in captivity for nearly one year.

Pocahontas was treated well. During her stay, she became interested in learning the ways of the English. She had already been exposed to their culture and language, as she had been a friend to them since her childhood. She was especially receptive to learning about Christianity. Around 1613, while she was still in captivity, Pocahontas was baptized. She took the Christian

This 1619 engraving by Theodore de Bry was based on a work by Georg Keller. Hoping to pressure Chief Powhatan into negotiating for Pocahontas's return, Sir Thomas Dale ordered a 1614 attack on a Powhatan village. A party of English colonists came ashore and burned several Powhatan homes and killed about five Powhatan warriors.

name of Rebecca. Pocahontas was the first Powhatan Indian to become a Christian.

By the beginning of 1614, Powhatan still had not paid the full ransom for his daughter. Finally, in March, Sir Thomas Dale took Pocahontas and a large group of men to Powhatan's new capital, Matchcot. Although Dale and his men were not able to speak directly with Powhatan, they were able to send him a message. While they were in Matchcot, two of Powhatan's sons asked to see Pocahontas and were pleased to see that their sister was

John Gadsby Chapman imagined the baptism of Pocahontas in his painting from around 1840. The minister Alexander Whitaker, shown standing before the kneeling Pocahontas, selected Rebecca as Pocahontas's baptismal name. In the Bible, Rebecca is a foreigner who comes to live with the Hebrew family of Abraham in Canaan.

well. The two brothers spoke with Pocahontas and promised to convince their father to make peace.

Sir Thomas Dale wrote in a 1614 letter, which was included in Ralph Hamor's 1615 *A True Discourse of the Present Estate of Virginia*, that Pocahontas was displeased, or possibly hurt, that her father had been so slow in negotiating her release. Dale, an eyewitness to this meeting, wrote, "The king's daughter went ashore but would not talk to any of them, scarce to them of the best sort, and to them only that if her father had loved her, he would not value her less than old swords, [guns], or axes; wherefore she would still dwell with the Englishmen, who loved her."

One of the men who accompanied Dale on that trip was John Rolfe, a twenty-eight-year-old widowed tobacco planter. Pocahontas, who was then about nineteen years old, had gotten to know Rolfe while she was in Jamestown and the two had fallen in love. Rolfe wanted to marry Pocahontas, but marriage between an English colonist and a Powhatan woman was unheard of. This simply had never happened before. Even though Pocahontas had learned English customs and had become a Christian, Europeans at that time still considered Native American peoples to be primitive. John Rolfe wrote a letter to Dale explaining his feelings about Pocahontas and requested Dale's advice.

During this trip to Matchcot, Rolfe asked one of the other colonists to take his letter to Dale. Dale approved of the marriage and Rolfe, Dale, and Pocahontas all returned to Jamestown. Powhatan heard of the marriage

John Rolfe planted a variety of tobacco seeds to test which seeds produced the best crop. Pocahontas helped Rolfe by teaching him techniques that the Powhatans used to grow tobacco.

plans from Pocahontas's two brothers and he, too, gave his approval of the union.

Pocahontas, like Rolfe, had also been married before. Rolfe was widowed when he met Pocahontas, but there is no record of what happened to Pocahontas's husband. Pocahontas had been married to a man named Kocoum in 1610 when she was still a young girl. Not much else is known about Kocoum except for his name and that he was described by the English as a "pryvate Captayn." However, it was common in Powhatan culture for people to consider themselves divorced when a spouse was kidnapped by an enemy. This is possibly what happened when the English kidnapped Pocahontas.

Elmer Boyd Smith depicted the wedding of Pocahontas and John Rolfe in 1906. Although Powhatan refused to attend the ceremony, he sent his daughter a freshwater pearl necklace as a gift. The bride wore a muslin tunic, a robe, and a veil that had been made in England.

In 1614, Ralph Hamor was sent to negotiate with Chief Powhatan on behalf of Sir Thomas Dale, who was interested in marrying one of the chief's daughters. Powhatan told Hamor that his daughter was pledged to marry another. Theodore de Bry based this 1619 engraving on an earlier work done by Georg Keller.

Pocahontas and John Rolfe were married in April 1614 in Jamestown. Although Powhatan did not attend the wedding, he kept peace with the English afterward. Powhatan was then in his midsixties, and he began to let his brothers take on the leadership of his people. The marriage of Pocahontas and John Rolfe brought an end to the First Anglo-Powhatan War.

In 1615, Pocahontas and John Rolfe had a son whom they named Thomas. The following year, in the spring of 1616, Pocahontas, John Rolfe, and Thomas set off on a trip to England. About twelve Powhatan people, including a priest named Uttamatomakkin, who was an

This is a painting of Pocahontas and her son Thomas Rolfe. In a 1617 letter, John Rolfe wrote to Sir Edwin Sandys that his son Thomas, who was then about one year old, closely resembled his mother.

adviser to Powhatan, accompanied the Rolfe family on their voyage. Powhatan had sent the adviser to learn about England and to see English people in their homeland. The group arrived in England in June.

When John Smith learned that Pocahontas was in England, he wrote a letter to Queen Anne. Smith described how Pocahontas had twice saved his life and had come to the aid of the Virginian colonists. Smith strongly recommended to the queen that Pocahontas be treated with respect, or "her present love to us and Christianity might turn to such scorn and fury. . . ."

Pocahontas met the nobility of English society and attended the court of King James I and Queen Anne. She was invited to attend a dramatic play, known as a masque, held at the king's court. At the masque Pocahontas sat in a place of honor that was reserved for special guests. As the daughter of a powerful ruler, Pocahontas was considered a princess and she was treated like royalty. During Pocahontas's stay in

England, the Virginia Company of London presented her as a success story for England's continued presence in the New World. Her transformation from a "savage" into an English lady made Pocahontas an example of how the English in Virginia were civilizing the Native American population.

During her time in England, Pocahontas learned that John Smith, the friend she thought long dead, was still alive. Pocahontas spent the last part of her visit in the country, in Middlesex, where Smith paid her a visit. Smith did not visit Pocahontas until she was about to return to Virginia. He later recounted their meeting in

Pocahontas met King James in 1616, an event that was dramatized in a 1907 print by Richard Rummels. The Reverend Samuel Purchas wrote in 1625 that Pocahontas was respected and well received in court because "she still carried her selfe as the daughter of a king."

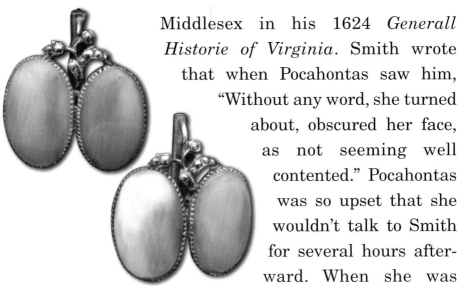

Pocahontas owned these double-shell earrings. The Earl of Northumberland, a friend of the Rolfes, was said to have set the shells in silver after Pocahontas paid him a visit in the Tower of London in 1617.

Middlesex in his 1624 *Generall Historie of Virginia*. Smith wrote that when Pocahontas saw him, "Without any word, she turned about, obscured her face, as not seeming well contented." Pocahontas was so upset that she wouldn't talk to Smith for several hours afterward. When she was finally composed enough to speak, she told him that the Jamestown colonists had told her that he was dead. Pocahontas scornfully told Smith, "Your Countriemen will lie much." Pocahontas never saw John Smith again.

In March 1617, Pocahontas and her husband and son boarded a ship to return to Virginia. According to a 1617 letter written by Sir John Chamberlain, Pocahontas would have preferred to remain in England.

The ship stopped at Gravesend, a town in Kent, England, to allow Pocahontas to be taken ashore. She had become extremely ill. Pocahontas died in Gravesend. The cause of Pocahontas's death was not recorded. She probably suffered from a respiratory ailment, or a problem with her lungs, such as tuberculosis or pneumonia. Before she passed away, Pocahontas comforted her husband, "All must die. Tis enough that the child liveth." John Rolfe noted his wife's final words in a June 8, 1617 letter.

Pocahontas was given a Christian burial at St. George's Church in Gravesend on March 21, 1617. In the following century, a fire destroyed the church and as the new church was being built, Pocahontas's grave was destroyed.

John Rolfe and his son Thomas set sail again for Virginia, but the boy soon became ill and was unable to make the voyage. At Plymouth, England, Thomas was left in the care of an uncle and was raised as an Englishman. John Rolfe returned to Virginia alone. Thomas Rolfe would later journey to Virginia, the place of his birth, in 1635. By that time his father, too, had died.

10. The Virginia Colony Continues to Grow

After Pocahontas's funeral, John Rolfe sailed back to Virginia on one of Samuel Argall's ships. Upon arrival in May 1617, Rolfe and Argall found that Jamestown was in poor condition. The buildings were in need of repair. The streets were being used to grow tobacco, which had become the main product the colonists exported for sale in Europe. Argall took control of the colony and tried to restore order.

The summer of 1617 was a sorrowful one for both the colonists and the Powhatans. An epidemic hit the region and many colonists and Indians died. The type of disease the population suffered from was not recorded. That same year was also a bad year for crops. Those people who did not die of disease were in danger of starving.

By this time Powhatan's rule had passed into the hands of his brothers, Opichapam and Opechancanough. At nearly seventy years old, Chief Powhatan died in April 1618. His brother, Opichapam, became the new supreme chief. However, Opichapam was not an active leader. In fact, it was Powhatan's other brother, Opechancanough,

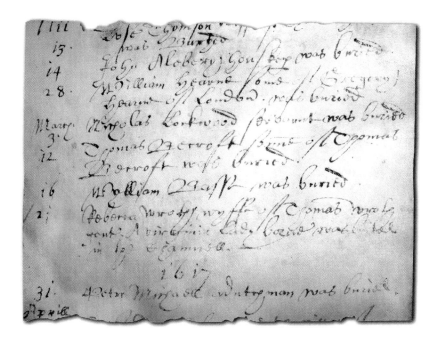

This church record from St. George's Church of Gravesend, England, documented the burial of Pocahontas on March 21, 1617. The entry for her death says that "Rebecca Wroth . . . a Virginia Lady borne was buried in the Chauncell." Pocahontas was probably buried beneath the chancel, an elevated area of the church that holds the altar, the choir, and the members of the clergy.

who had the real power and who made all the decisions for the Powhatan nation.

Although there had been peace between the colonists and the Powhatans in the years since Pocahontas and John Rolfe had married, the colonists remained wary of the Powhatans. The English were outnumbered by the Indians. This remained true even though the colony's population had begun to grow. The successful industry of growing tobacco in Virginia inspired many more English people to go there in search of profit. In April 1618, there were 400 colonists in Virginia, and one year

This image depicts colonists harvesting tobacco in Jamestown. The export of tobacco increased dramatically within the first few years of its cultivation in Virginia. In March 1614, John Rolfe was the first colonist to ship four barrels of tobacco to England. By 1618, Virginian colonists had shipped almost 50,000 pounds of tobacco to England.

later there were almost 1,000. By 1621, the English colonists had taken over about one-half of the original area of Powhatan's territory.

The peace brought about by Pocahontas's marriage to John Rolfe lasted until 1622. Not only were the English colonists taking over Powhatan territory at an alarming rate, but also the Powhatans were offended by the colonists' repeated attempts to convert them to Christianity.

The colonists frequently pressured Indian parents to send their children to English settlements. The children could then be raised in what the English considered to be the proper way.

On the morning of March 22, 1622,

In summer 2003, a team of archaeologists began excavation on a Virginian farm owned by Lynn and Bob Ripley. The farm is believed to be located on the site of Werowocomoco, the main residence of Chief Powhatan and the Powhatans of coastal Virginia during the early 1600s. The Ripleys contacted authorities when they discovered artifacts such as pottery and arrowheads on their property.

Archaeologists work by removing dirt from small sections of land. The dirt is then sifted and inspected for artifacts. Among the numerous finds on the Ripley's farm have been blue glass beads that were probably made in Europe in the 1600s. According to an account written by John Smith, the colonists traded blue beads for corn during their first winter at Jamestown.

Opechancanough launched an attack against the colonists of Virginia. About one-quarter of the settlement's population was killed. John Rolfe, who died sometime in 1622, might have been one of the people killed in the assault. The attack came as a surprise to most of the colonists, although some of them had been warned beforehand by sympathetic Indians. Even though the colonists had still been cautious of the Powhatans, they had felt that the relationship between them was friendly. Indians had gone freely about the English settlements to trade, and some Powhatans had

This 1628 engraving by Matthaeus Merian depicts the 1622 Second Anglo-Powhatan War. The loss of life from the March 22, 1622, attack crushed the morale of the colonists. William Capps wrote in a 1623 letter, "I thinke the last massacre killed all our countrie. . . . Beside them they killed, they burst the heart of all the rest."

even worked for the English tobacco planters. Therefore, many of the settlers were shocked by the attack.

This act of violence started the second major war between the English and the Powhatan Indians. Opechancanough was certain that the English would finally leave Virginia for good when so many colonists were killed. This did not happen, however. Instead, the English retaliated, or took revenge, with more violence and continued to send additional colonists to Virginia. In 1646, Opechancanough, who was at least eighty years old, was captured. He was later killed by the soldier assigned to guard him. Virginia was entirely under English control.

11. The Algonquian Indians of Virginia

Jamestown was the first capital of Virginia and was the site where the colonists established Europe's first assembly of representatives in the New World. The General Assembly met for the first time on July 30, 1619, to form a single governing body throughout the settlements of the Virginia Colony. The General Assembly was created to provide "just laws for the happy guiding and governing of the people there inhabiting."

In the same year, the first Africans arrived in Jamestown to work as the indentured servants of the Jamestown planters. As the cultivation and export of tobacco increased in Virginia, the planters needed additional workers. Tobacco plants required an enormous amount of labor and the economic advantage of an unpaid workforce spurred the growth of slavery in Virginia. By the 1680s, Africans were no longer brought to America as indentured servants. Instead, they were captured and then sold in the colonies as slaves.

In 1624, King James I took control of Virginia away from the Virginia Company and made Virginia a royal colony. Jamestown remained the capital of Virginia until 1698, when a fire destroyed the statehouse. The following year, the capital was moved to Williamsburg and the town of Jamestown fell into decay.

• • • •

Today Jamestown is part of the Colonial National Historical Park. The site, which was acquired by the

The Pamunkey, a people that were once part of Powhatan's chiefdom, help to restore the supply of shad fish in Virginia's bays and rivers. In hatcheries, such as the one shown here, shad eggs are hatched and raised in vats. The young shad are later released into Virginia's waterways.

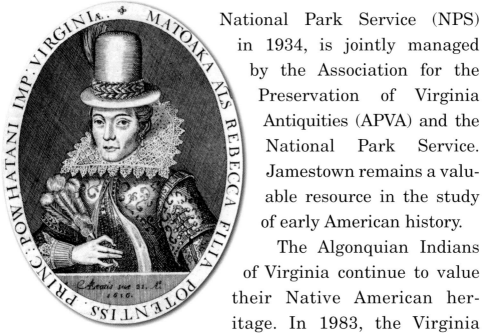

This Simon van de Passe 1616 engraving is believed to be the most accurate representation of what Pocahontas actually looked like. The decorative ostrich plume that she holds was considered a sign of wealth. At the base of the image, the artist recorded Pocahontas's age in 1616 as twenty-one.

National Park Service (NPS) in 1934, is jointly managed by the Association for the Preservation of Virginia Antiquities (APVA) and the National Park Service. Jamestown remains a valuable resource in the study of early American history.

The Algonquian Indians of Virginia continue to value their Native American heritage. In 1983, the Virginia Council on Indians was established to serve as a link between the native peoples of Virginia and the state government. This organization ensures that the voice of the Native American community is heard when decisions are made on important matters affecting all citizens in Virginia. There are eight tribal groups in Virginia today: the Chickahominy, Chickahominy Eastern Division, Mattaponi, Nansemond, Pamunkey, Rappahannock, Upper Mattaponi, and Monacan. All but the Monacan were part of Powhatan's original chiefdom.

In 1914, the Colonial Dames of America, a group that promotes American heritage, presented this stained glass Pocahontas memorial to St. George's Church in Gravesend, England. The central image is the biblical figure Rebecca. The cartouche, or pictorial inset, at the bottom of the window portrays the baptism of Pocahontas.

William Ordway Partridge unveiled his bronze statue of Pocahontas for Jamestown Island, Virginia, in 1922. The period of calm that followed her marriage to John Rolfe was known by the Jamestown colonists as the Peace of Pocahontas. The artist depicted Pocahontas wearing clothes that were more representative of a Plains Indian, rather than a Powhatan from the Chesapeake Bay area of Virginia.

Nearly four centuries after her death, Pocahontas is still remembered as a beloved figure in American history. Pocahontas never wrote about her own life, so we can only come to know her through the accounts of others. Yet the stories that were written by those who did know her show an admiration for the child Pocahontas once was and for the woman she became. She is remembered today, as she was by the Jamestown colonists, as a bright and gracious person who did all she could to bridge the gap between cultures in conflict.

Timeline

**Mid-1500s
to 1607** Chief Powhatan inherits several Indian groups and expands his domain to create a paramount chiefdom.

About 1560 Spain attempts to establish a colony in the Chesapeake Bay area, along the southeastern coast of North America.

1584 England fails in the attempt to establish a colony on Roanoke Island off the coast of present-day North Carolina.

1587 A second attempt is made to establish a colony on Roanoke and succeeds, but the colony is found deserted in 1590.

About 1595 Pocahontas is born.

1606 In April, King James I of England grants a charter to the Virginia Company to start a colony in North America.

On December 20, the *Susan Constant*, *Discovery*, and *Godspeed* set sail from England carrying the first colonists to Jamestown.

1607 In April, the English arrive in Virginia and begin exploring the area. On May 13, the colonists arrive at James Island and begin building a settlement they call Jamestown.

In June, Powhatan sends a message to the colonists saying he wants to establish a peaceful relationship.

In December, Smith is captured by an Indian hunting party led by Powhatan's brother Opechancanough. Later, Smith meets Powhatan for the first time.

1608	In January, Smith is released from captivity and returns to Jamestown.
	John Smith writes *True Relation*, in which he tells how Pocahontas first came to Jamestown as her father's messenger.
	In September, Smith is chosen president of the Jamestown Colony.
1609	In January, Powhatan invites Smith to his capital to trade for food to give to the starving colonists. At the end of the visit, Smith and his men escape a trap to kill them, and Powhatan flees to another town.
	In September, Smith is injured in a gunpowder explosion. He is removed from his leadership position in the colony.
	On October 4, Smith leaves Jamestown and returns to England.
1609–1610	Many colonists die during the Starving Time in Virginia.
1609–1614	The First Anglo-Powhatan War is fought.
1610	The colonists attempt to abandon Jamestown in the spring but turn around when they meet a supply ship on its way to Virginia.
1613	Pocahontas is kidnapped by Captain Argall and is held for ransom for nearly one year in Jamestown.
	Pocahontas is baptized a Christian and takes the name Rebecca.
1614	Pocahontas marries John Rolfe.
1616	Pocahontas travels to England in the spring and is introduced into English society.
1617	While in England, Pocahontas dies on March 21. She is buried in St. George's Church, Gravesend.

Glossary

Algonquian (al-GAHN-kwee-un) A family of languages spoken by the native peoples of Virginia and other areas of North America.

archaeological (ar-kee-uh-LA-jih-kul) Having to do with the study of the way humans lived long ago.

artifacts (AR-tih-fakts) Objects created and produced by humans.

baptized (BAP-tyzd) To have sprinkled someone with or to have immersed someone in water to show that person's acceptance into the Christian faith.

brackish (BRA-kish) Somewhat salty.

charter (CHAR-tur) An official agreement giving someone permission to do something.

chiefdom (CHEEF-dom) A kind of government made up of several towns or villages brought together under one ruler or chief.

coronation (kor-uh-NAY-shun) A ceremony in which a king or queen is publicly recognized as a ruler.

dialect (DY-uh-lekt) A kind of language spoken only in a certain area.

epidemic (eh-pih-DEH-mik) The quick spreading of a sickness so that many people have it at the same time.

estuary (ES-choo-wehr-ee) An area of water where the ocean tide meets a river.

exploitation (ek-sploy-TAY-shun) An act or instance of making productive use of something to one's own advantage.

exported (ek-SPORT-ed) Sent out for trade or sale.

finance (feh-NANS) To back up with money.

indentured servants (in-DEN-churd SER-vints) People who have worked for other people for a fixed amount of time for payment of travel or living costs.

interaction (in-ter-AK-shun) Action or communication between people.

intimidating (in-TIH-muh-dayt-ing) Frightening or threatening.

Jesuit (JEH-shyoo-wit) Relating to a Roman Catholic religious order that is officially called the Society of Jesus. It was founded in 1534 by St. Ignatius Loyola.

mamanatowick (ma-man-a-TOW-ik) The supreme leader of the Powhatan Indians.

masque (MASK) A dramatic play.

mercenary (MER-suh-ner-ee) Any professional soldier serving in a foreign army for pay.

moored (MOORD) Fixed in place by an anchor.

mortars (MOR-turz) Strong bowls in which things are pounded or rubbed into powder and paste.

nonpareil (non-puh-REL) Someone who stands above everyone else; a person who is unequaled.

novelties (NAH-vul-teez) New and interesting items.

pestles (PEH-sulz) Tools used to pound things into powder and paste.

quiyoughcosuck (kwee-YOO-ah-suk) Powhatan priests.

rushes (RUSH-ez) Grasslike plants that grow near water.

treacherous (TREH-chuh-rus) False, faithless, or dangerous.

tribute (TRIH-byoot) Payment made to a ruler by his or her people as a show of respect.

ventures (VEN-churz) Undertakings that involve risk or danger.

weroance (WER-o-wans) A male Powhatan chief of a town or smaller chiefdom.

weroansqua (wer-o-WAN-skwah) A female Powhatan chief.

yeoman (YOH-men) A person who owns and takes care of a small farm.

Additional Resources

If you would like to learn more about Pocahontas and the Powhatan culture, check out the following books and Web sites:

Books

Feest, Christian F. *The Powhatan Tribes*. New York: Chelsea House Publishers, 1990.

Sullivan, George. *Pocahontas*. New York: Scholastic Reference, 2002.

Web Sites

Due to the changing nature of Internet links, PowerPlus Books has developed an online list of Web sites related to the subject of this book. This site is updated regularly. Please use this link to access the list: www.powerkidslinks.com/lalt/pocahontas/

Bibliography

American Indian Resource Center, Department of Anthropology, College of William and Mary, Williamsburg, Virginia: www.wm.edu/AIRC

The Association for the Preservation of Virginia Antiquities, Jamestown Rediscovery: www.apva.org

Essential Documents in American History, Essential Documents 1492–Present. Complied by Norman P. Desmarais and James H. McGovern of Providence College. Property of Great Neck Publishing. Obtained online through Academic Search Premier.

Feest, Christian F. *The Powhatan Tribes.* New York: Chelsea House Publishers, 1990.

Gilliam, Charles Edgar. *"His Dearest Daughter's Names,"* in *William and Mary College Quarterly Historical Magazine,* Second Series, Volume 21, Issue 3 (July 1941), pp. 239–242.

Hawke, David Freeman, ed. *Captain John Smith's History of Virginia; A Selection.* Modern English version. Indianapolis and New York: The Bobbs-Merrill Company, Inc., 1970.

Hulton, Paul. *America, 1585: The Complete Drawings of John White.* Chapel Hill, North Carolina: The University of North Carolina Press, 1984.

Mossiker, Frances. *Pocahontas: The Life and the Legend.* New York: Knopf, 1976.

Price, David A. *Love and Hate in Jamestown.* New York: Alfred A. Knopf, 2003.

Quitt, Martin H. *"Trade and Acculturation at Jamestown, 1607–1609: The Limits of Understanding,"* in *The William and Mary Quarterly,* Third Series, Volume 52, Issue 2 (April 1995), pp. 227–258.

Robertson, Karen. *"Pocahontas at the Masque,"* in *Signs: Journal of Women in Culture & Society,* Spring 1996, Volume 21, Issue 3, pp. 551–583.

Rountree, Helen. *Pocahontas's People: The Powhatan Indians of Virginia Through Four Centuries.* Norman, Oklahoma: University of Oklahoma Press, 1990.

———. *The Powhatan Indians of Virginia: Their Traditional Culture.* Norman, Oklahoma: University of Oklahoma Press, 1989.

———. *"Who Were the Powhatans and Did They Have a Unified 'Foreign Policy',"* and *"The Powhatans and the English: A Case of Multiple Conflicting Agendas,"* in *Powhatan Foreign Relations 1500–1722,* edited by Helen Rountree, pp. 1–19 and pp. 173–205. Charlottesville, Virginia: University Press of Virginia, 1993.

Rountree, Helen and E. Randolph Turner, III. *Before and After Jamestown: Virginia's Powhatans and Their Predecessors.* Gainesville, Florida: University Press of Florida, 2002.

Smith, Bradford. *Captain John Smith: His Life and Legend.* Philadelphia and New York: J.B. Lippincott Company, 1953.

Turner, E. Randolph, III. *"Native American Protohistoric Interactions in the Powhatan Core Area,"* in *Powhatan Foreign Relations 1500–1722,* edited by Helen Rountree, pp. 76-93. Charlottesville, Virginia: University Press of Virginia, 1993.

Virtual Jamestown: www.iath.virginia.edu/vcdh/jamestown

Woodward, Grace Steele. *Pocahontas.* Norman, Oklahoma: University of Oklahoma Press, 1969.

Index

About the Author

Lisa Sita is a curriculum developer at the La Guardia and Wagner Archives of La Guardia Community College, City University of New York. Before joining City University, Sita worked in the field of museum education as a programs coordinator, teaching anthropology and American history. She has a Master's degree in anthropology, with a specialization in Native American studies. Sita has written several children's books on multicultural topics, science, and history. She has coauthored two other books in the Library of American Lives and Times series, *Peter Stuyvesant* and *Nathan Hale*.

Primary Sources

Editorial Notes: Many of John White's Native American images are of the Secotan Indians from the late 1500s. Powhatan images from that time in Virginia were not preserved. A choice was made to use images of the nearby North Carolina Secotan Indians, who were culturally related to the Powhatans. In the 1950s, the National Parks Department commissioned Sidney E. King to create a series of Jamestown images, including the ones that appear on pages 38, 73, 81, and 90. All the images were based on period artifacts and primary source paintings and drawings.

Cover. Rebecca Rolfe, oil painting. An unidentified artist based the image on a 1616 engraving by Simon van de Passe, Getty; Background: *The Abduction of Pocahontas*, engraving, 1619, Theodore de Bry, based on an earlier work by Georg Keller, Library of Congress, Rare Book and Special Collections Division. **Page 4.** (See cover.) **Page 8.** *Woman and Child of Pomeiooc*, watercolor, circa 1585, John White, British Museum, London, UK. **Page 12.** *Indian Village of Secoton*, watercolor, 1585, John White, British Museum, London, UK. **Page 16.** *Indians Fishing*, watercolor, 1585, John White, British Museum, London, UK. **Page 18.** *Cooking in a Pot*, watercolor, nineteenth century, Mrs. P. D. H. Page, based on an a watercolor by John White, Yale Center for British Art, Paul Mellon Collection, USA. **Page 19.** Deerskin bag decorated with shell beads, circa 1614, Virginia Powhatans, courtesy of the Visitors of the Ashmolean Museum, Oxford, UK. **Page 20.** *Indian Woman, one of the wives of Wyngyne*, watercolor, 1585, John White, British Museum, London, UK. **Page 22.** *Indians Dancing*. This image may depict a green corn or harvest festival, which was celebrated by the Secotan Indians when the first ears of maize, or Indian corn, were harvested. Watercolor, 1585, John White, British Museum, London, UK. **Page 23.** *Indian Priest*, watercolor, 1585, John White, British Museum, London, UK. **Page 26.** Powhatan, image appears on John Smith's 1608 Map of Virginia, engraving [coloring of image is modern]. Although this version of the image was published in London in 1624, William Hole first created the engraving in 1612, Library of Congress Geography and Map Division. **Page 28.** Powhatan's mantle, deerskin cloak decorated with shells that was worn by Chief Powhatan or another chief, late 1500s or early 1600s, courtesy of the Visitors of the Ashmolean Museum, Oxford, UK. **Page 32.** Charter for the Virginia Company of London, 1606, authorized by King James I in 1606, parchment, Library of Congress, Manuscript Division. **Pages 34–35.** *Virginia, Discovered and Discribed by Captayn John Smith*, engraving [coloring of map is modern]. Smith created his map of Virginia in 1608, which was based on his exploration of the region around 1607, this version of the map was published in London in 1624, William Hole, Library of Congress Geography and Map Division. **Page 36.** Glass beads, circa 1500s, probably created in the Venetian Republic. Trading beads such as these were given to the English colonists before they left Europe. Historical records indicate that blue beads were the most appealing to Chief Powhatan because they were the color of the sky. Courtesy of APVA (The Association for the Preservation of Virginia Antiquities). **Page 40.** *The Settlers at Virginia*, engraving, 1876, W.L.S., Print Collection, Miriam and Ira D. Wallach Division of Art, Prints and Photographs, New York Public

Library, Astor, Lenox, and Tilden Foundations. **Page 43.** *The Generall Historie of Virginia, New-England, and the Summer Isles*, title page, John Smith, 1624, courtesy of the Rare Books & Manuscripts Collection, New York Public Library, Astor, Lenox, and Tilden Foundations. **Page 47.** *Captian John Smith, 1st Governor of Virginia*, oil painting, circa 1616, unknown artist. **Page 49.** Dutch Musketeer, illustration from *The Exercise of Armes*, engraving, published in Amsterdam in 1608, Jacob de Gheyn, Anne S.K. Brown Military Collection. **Page 53**. *A True Relation of such occurrences and accidents of noate as hath hapned in Virginia since the first planting of that Collony, which is now resident in the South part thereof, till the last returne from thence*, title page, published in London in 1608, John Smith, courtesy of the Rare Books & Manuscripts Collection, New York Public Library, Astor, Lenox, and Tilden Foundations. **Page 54.** *Pocahontas Saving the Life of Captain John Smith*, oil painting, circa 1836, John Gadsby Chapman, New-York Historical Society, New York. **Page 59.** Replica of a late-1500s basket-hilt broadsword, forged steel blade, steel basket, wood and wire grip, leather and red wool liner, courtesey of Luther Sowers, Salisbury, NC. **Page 62.** *King James I of England*, oil painting, circa 1610, Paul van Somer, Prado Museum, Spain. **Page 69.** Coat of Arms of the Virginia Company of London, 1633, engraving, courtesy of the Rare Books & Manuscripts Collection, New York Public Library, Astor, Lenox, and Tilden Foundations. **Page 70.** A Chart of Virginia, ink and pigment on vellum, circa 1607, The Phelps Stokes Collection, Miriam and Ira D. Wallach Division of Art, Prints and Photographs, New York Public Library, Astor, Lenox, and Tilden Foundations. **Page 74.** *Thomas West, 12th Baron, Lord De La Warr*, oil painting, 1882, Margaret Thomas. The artist based her work on an earlier painting created by Wybrand Simonsz de Geest. **Page 77.** *The Abduction of Pocahontas*, engraving, 1619, Theodore de Bry, based on an earlier work by Georg Keller, Library of Congress, Rare Book and Special Collections Division. **Page 79.** This is a detailed close-up from the Theodore de Bry engraving that appears on the cover and on page 77, please see previous entry. **Page 80.** *Baptism of Pocahontas*, oil painting, circa 1840, John Gadsby Chapman, painting located in the rotunda of the U.S. Capitol. **Page 83.** *Ralph Hamor visits Powahatan with a proposal*, engraving, 1619, Theodore de Bry. The artist based his engraving on an earlier work done by Georg Keller, Library of Congress, Rare Book and Special Collections Division. **Page 84.** Pocahontas and her son Thomas Rolfe, oil painting, circa 1800. The painting was done by an artist of the American school and is believed to be a copy of an earlier original. The painting is on permanent loan to the Town Hall of King's Lynn and West Norfolk. **Page 86.** Pocahontas's double-shell earrings. The shells were set in a silver jewelry design created by the Earl of Northumberland, circa 1617, courtesy of APVA Preservation Virginia. **Page 89.** The March 21, 1617, entry from the parish register of St. George's Church, Gravesend, England, which documents the burial of "Rebecca Wroth," courtesy of the Rector and Parochial Church Council of St. George's Church, Gravesend, Kent and the Director of Education and Leisure, Medway Council, Kent, UK. **Page 92.** *The 1622 Second Anglo-Powhatan War*, engraving, 1628, Matthaeus Merian, image rights owned by the Virginia Historical Society. **Page 96.** Pocahontas. This is the only known life portrait of Pocahontas, engraving, 1616, Simon van de Passe, Library of Congress, Rare Books and Special Collections Division.

Credits

Photo Credits

Cover, p. 4 © Hulton/Archive/Getty Images; p. 7 © The New York Public Library / Art Resource, NY; p. 8 British Museum, London/Bridgeman Art Library; pp. 11, 15 Courtesy, Robert Llewellyn, Charlottesville, VA; 12, 16, 20, 22, 23, 47, Private Collection/Bridgeman Art Library; p. 18 © Yale Center for British Art, Paul Mellon Collection/Bridgeman Art Library; pp. 19, 28 by courtesy of the Visitors of the Ashmolean Museum, Oxford, UK; pp. 26, 34-35, Library of Congress, Geography and Map Division; p. 29 The Mariners' Museum, Newport News, VA; p. 32 Library of Congress, Manuscript Division; pp. 36, 98 Courtesy of APVA Preservation Virginia; pp. 38, 73, 90 National Park Service, Colonial National Historical Park; pp. 40, 82 Print Collection, Miriam and Ira D. Wallach Division of Art, Prints, and Photographs, New York Public Library Astor, Lenox, and Tilden Foundations; pp. 43, 53, 69 Rare Books & Manuscripts Collection, New York Public Library Astor, Lenox, and Tilden Foundations; p. 49 Anne S. K. Brown Military Collection, Brown University Library; p. 54 © New-York Historical Society/Bridgeman Art Library; p. 59 Courtesy of Luther Sowers, Salisbury, NC; p. 62 Prado, Madrid, Spain/Bridgeman Art Library; p. 70 the Phelps Stokes Collection, Miriam and Ira D. Wallach Division of Art, Prints, and Photographs, the New York Public Library, Astor Lenox, and Tilden Foundations; p. 74 Courtesy Independence National Historical Park; pp. 76, 79, 83, 96 Library of Congress, Rare Book and Special Collections Division; p. 80 Architect of the Capitol; p. 81 Courtesy of the Jamestown-Yorktown Educational Trust; p. 84 Photo by David Pitcher with permission of the Borough Council of King's Lynn and West Norfolk; p. 85 Library of Congress, Prints and Photographs Division; p. 86 Courtesy of APVA Preservation Virginia, photography by Katherine Wetzel; p. 89 Courtesy of the Rector and Parochial Church Council of St. George's Church, Gravesend, Kent and the Director of Education and Leisure, Medway Council, Kent, U.K.; p. 92 the Virginia Historical Society, Richmond, VA; p. 95 Courtesy, U.S. Fish and Wildlife Service; p. 97 with kind permission of St. George's Church, Gravesend, Kent, U.K./photo by Alan Kelly, London, U.K.

Project Editor
Daryl Heller

Series Design
Laura Murawski

Layout Design
Ginny Chu

Photo Researcher
Jeffrey Wendt